"I am deeply amazed at
and make it so easily ur
evant and practical. When applied, the principles he shares will
help create true men and women of God, regardless of their
field or calling."

Dutch Sheets
Pastor and Author

"In *Leadership Journey*, Dr. Alemu Beeftu has captured a valuable
life-long perspective on Christian leadership. Each stage of development
in the life of a leader is filled with potential and peril.
Dr. Beeftu helps the reader begin well, continue well and finish
well in his or her personal leadership journey."

Don Steiger, Sr. Pastor
Bethel Church of San Jose, California

"Leadership that lacks a deep and personal relationship with the
living God is without the most powerful ingredient in the business.
Leadership Journey is a book that is born from a genuine
conviction that leaders can make a difference, once they are enlightened
by the truth of God. It leads leaders into the position
of a servant's attitude and challenges them to evaluate the purpose
of it all.

"This is a handbook for every servant of the King and His kingdom.
I know Dr. Beeftu and his family in the privacy of their
home, as well as in public life. This book simply reflects his deep
commitment to the Word of God and body of Christ in whatever
he does. Dr. Beeftu makes leadership, according to the book,
most enjoyable to read and achievable in practicing it."

Dr. Tolesa Gudina
Founder & President of Truth in Love Ministry
and Pastor in Atlanta, Georgia

"If there is one topic that has enough material written about it, it is leadership. What is special about this book is that it comes as a mirror to the reader and constantly challenges him to evaluate not the concept of leadership, but his own life and calling from different penetrating angles. It makes you restless and anxious as you see your shortfalls – but also rested and believing when you realize that 'He who began a good work in you will carry it on to completion.'

"The concepts presented are simple but profound, down to earth and practical. To the sincere reader, the temptation to get 'a new idea' to pass on to someone becomes irrelevant. I am face to face with God and what I am doing with my call in life – whether I am young and ready for battle, or whether I am older and ready to pass on the baton."

Dr. Betta Mengistu
Executive Director of Africa Area,
International Bible Society

"While Alemu Beeftu was completing his graduate work at Michigan State University, I became acquainted with him and soon realized he was the kind of staff Compassion International needed. We were blessed by the passion and effectiveness of this gifted and dedicated man of God.

"It is appropriate for Alemu Beeftu to write this book on the development of Christian leaders. His life's passion and calling has been to help grow future leaders of the Church in the developing world. His text is a unique blend of biblical characters and how they responded and manifested leadership under God's direction, experiences of Christian leaders in today's western culture and his own insights."

Wally Erickson
Former President of Compassion International

"As a businessman who has had the opportunity to be involved in a ministry to advance the kingdom of God, I have stated for many years that I did this as a volunteer because I had never heard a call from God. *Leadership Journey* has greatly impacted me. I was moved to tears. I realize that God has called me, and I am so inspired by the creative way Dr. Beeftu has presented this. I applaud him for his unique and creative approach to finding God's will for our lives and letting that determine our adventure in leadership opportunities and successes."

David Burdine
Former President of Bethesda Associates

"Dr. Alemu Beeftu's book, *Leadership Journey*, is an excellent manual for Christian leaders. It instructs, challenges and gives hope. His practical application to biblical principles covers many aspects in one's journey in developing leadership skills. The book was birthed from Dr. Beeftu's vast experience in teaching leadership courses. The reader soon appreciates his depth of understanding the myriad issues involved in mentoring leaders. I believe you will be glad you read it. I know I was blessed by it."

Quin Sherrer
Author of Listen, God is Speaking to You

"Rooted deeply in Scripture and grounded in vast experience, Dr. Beeftu insightfully portrays leadership as a journey with distinctive features along the way. From the journey metaphor emerge principles of leadership that, unlike many books, are transcultural in application. With artistic skill, the author crafts the work so that it speaks equally to those who have positional leadership and those who do leadership tasks as part of their daily routine. Thus, a wide range of readers will benefit."

Duane Elmer
Trinity International University

"Most of the extensive bode of literature labeled 'leadership' gives little attention to the assumptions on which its axioms, models and standards are based. Alemu Beeftu takes a step back and guides the reader through an examination of some basic assumptions about one's path to leadership, God's intended leadership development program and the areas in which one's growth as a leader are to be measured. *Leadership Journey* is a practical resource for godly leaders at any stage in their walk with the Lord."

Paul Nelson
Executive Director, The Crowell Trust

"Alemu Beeftu and I have been fellow pilgrims on the leadership journey for many years. I am thankful for the way God has used him in my life and the lives of many others. I see in this book the wisdom that has shaped Dr. Beeftu's leadership, and I'm glad he has written it. In these days when effective leadership is desperately needed, I pray that *Leadership Journey* will strengthen thousands of men and women around the world."

James Plueddemann
President, Serving in Mission (SIM).

The LEADERSHIP JOURNEY

STRATEGIC LEADERSHIP FOR MAXIMUM IMPACT

ALEMU BEEFTU, PH.D.

Cool Springs Publishing House
Chicago, Illinois · Colorado Springs, Colorado

THE LEADERSHIP JOURNEY
© 2004 by Alemu Beeftu

All rights reserved. Except for brief excerpts for review purposes, no part of this book may be reproduced or used in any form without written permission from the publisher.

Unless otherwise noted, Scripture quotations in this publication are from the *Holy Bible, New International Version*. Copyright © 1973, 1978, 1984, International Bible Society. Used by permission of Zondervan Publishing House. All rights reserved.

ISBN 1-889860-03-4

First printing, 2004
Printed in **U.S.A.**

Dedication

I am honored to dedicate this book
—and to express my heartfelt gratitude—
to
Mulatu & Karin Belachew,
Bryant & Lisa Myers and
Wess & Donna Stafford
for their ongoing contributions
to my personal journey.

Acknowledgements

First, I am eternally grateful to God for His grace and the opportunity to serve Him in this manner.

I thank the Lord for my family. Genet, you are a helpmeet and partner far beyond what I ever imagined God would give me. Keah and Amman, your support and sacrifices mean more to me than you will ever know. I am proud to be your father.

I am also in debt to Judy Miller. Judy, you keep the Gospel of Glory office running smoothly and help me stay on schedule. Those two achievements are daily miracles. Thank you for being such a servant!

Steve Wamberg has been a special friend and a great editor to me. Pastor Mesfin Mamo set up this book and brought a fresh vision for the *Leadership Journey* diagram. The leaders who shared their personal experiences to make this book richer are the heart of this project. There are many others who have given their resources and lifted me up in prayer. For each of you, I bless God.

Contents

Foreword .... *i*
Introduction .... *iii*

Stage 1: The Calling 1
Discovering Your Call 4
Discovering the Dimensions of God's Call 15

Stage 2: Accepting the Call 23
Receiving the Pass 26
Accepting the Challenge 34

Stage 3: Early Leadership Stage 55
Needing to Lead and Succeed 58
Meeting Early Leadership Challenges 64

Stage 4: Reality Stage 81
Taking a Long, Hard Look at Yourself 84
Letting God Mold, Build, and Strengthen Your Character 92

Stage 5: Maturity Stage 107
Getting Your Hands Dirty 110
Setting the Example – Under Authority 123

Stage 6: Value Stage 139
Shaping History 142
Passing on Values 150

Stage 7: Relational Stage 163
Come and Fellowship 166
Finishing from Glory to Glory 174

Foreword

So, you have two questions about this book:
- Not another book on leadership!?!
- Who is Alemu Beeftu?

Your first observation is partially correct. There are literally hundreds of titles published dealing with leadership. One of the reasons for this prolific expansion of leadership titles is the almost insatiable demand by readers of all ages and professions to learn as much as they can on this topic. *This is because everyone is a current or future leader.* D.R. David put it this way:

> *Contrary to popular perception, a leader is not just the one at the top of the organization chart. Anyone who has the ability to influence how others think, feel and act can exercise a form of leadership. Anyone who is calling others to follow him as he/she follows Jesus is a leader.*

And so there is a huge, hungry audience who are aware that they influence others and seem desperate to know more.

Why is this book different? Two words in the above quote separate this book from 90 percent of the leadership books on the market today. The two words are "follows Jesus."

Now this brings us to the second point in the opening paragraph. Alemu Beeftu not only follows Jesus, he knows how to delve into the Scriptures to unlock the principles of leadership and how to apply them to our own situations and personality. Alemu presents these biblical principles and applications through the wisdom and discerning power of the Holy Spirit.

Alemu grew up as one of 10 children on an isolated farm in Ethiopia. He learned to read and write in a missionary school at the age of 12. As he grew up, his Christian friends encouraged him to travel to the US to escape the Communist government in power in the 1970s. He did so and earned a bachelors degree from Biola University and a masters and doctoral degree from Michigan State University. He founded his own ministry, Gospel of Glory, and through this ministry God called Alemu to equip and encourage leaders in developing countries—and now, in the western world.

It is rare, indeed, that anyone can tell us about leadership from a truly global perspective. I encourage you to take advantage of the hard-earned experience of the leaders Alemu brings to light in this book, and to reflect on the insights God has given Alemu about the lifetime process of biblical leadership. Alemu Beeftu is eminently and uniquely qualified to bring a fresh, Spirit-filled approach to this very important topic of leadership.

Peter Bradley
President, International Bible Society

Introduction

God has granted me great favor in allowing me, for more than 25 years, to help – and be mentored by – choice leaders. I have learned much from walking alongside these friends. Chief among the lessons I have learned is this: Leadership is a *journey* with purpose and destiny. It's a *process* one travels that builds character and life skills *under God's tutelage* to make a person into a more effective leader each stage of the way.

Leadership is life. Life is leadership. You can't divorce one from the other. That makes leadership a practical, daily undertaking. It is far more than a theoretical concept. In fact, most leaders are challenged by bringing the high calling of leadership to bear on everyday life. Leadership is indeed a journey of valleys and mountaintops. Biblical leaders like Joseph and Jeremiah found themselves in the pits (literally!) as a result of their calling, while others like Moses, Peter, James and John truly knew mountaintop experiences.

Because the leadership journey is a process, it also has identifiable stages. God uses each stage for character building, as well as for affirming His presence in the life of a leader. *The Leadership Journey* focuses on seven distinct stages of leadership:

- The Calling Stage
- Accepting the Call
- Early Leadership Stage
- Reality Stage
- Maturity Stage
- Value Stage
- Relational Stage

In the pages that follow, we'll examine principles, real-life examples and characters and events from the Bible that help define effective leadership – and all with a purpose:

- To merge together the Western view of leadership, the reality of the developing world and biblical truth for effective leadership.
- To balance leadership theory with practical applications.
- To present leadership as a lifetime process for growth and development.
- To help you balance leadership methods, paradigms and vision in everyday life.
- To encourage you personally toward a healthy leadership matrix that includes a sound mind, loving heart and clear vision.
- To provide a roadmap of the leadership process for emerging leaders. (In fact, you can see that roadmap on the following page.)
- To help experienced leaders evaluate and reflect on how well their leadership journey has progressed – and where it is taking them as they prepare to finish.
- To challenge those who are struggling with a call to leadership to start well on solid ground.
- To encourage those who are on the journey to finish well.

"Finishing well" as a leader is like running a race: You need a good start, and then you must run the course with a clear focus. This is my prayer for you as you pursue your own leadership journey: *That you have a good start, a clear focus and that you finish well.*

My prayer for this book is that somehow it will help you accomplish all of those things.

Alemu Beeftu

Stage 1
The Leadership Journey

I The Call
Process of >Hearing >Discerning >Promise >From, to and for

II Acceptance
Process of >Step of faith >Entering >Commission >Confirmation >Signs

III Early Leadership
Process of >History >Ministry >People >Team

IV Reality
Process of >Character building >Self discovery >Facing reality
>Personal gifts >Call >God >Knowledge

V Maturity
Process of >Building Ministry >Recognizing offices >Correcting History
>Making History >Shaping History

VI Value Stage
Process of >Relationship >Building people >Becoming a father
>Bearing Fruit >Establishing Pattern

VII Relational Stage
Process of >Relationship >Leaving a legacy

I The Call
Process of
>Hearing
>Discerning
>Promise
 >From, to and for

THE CALLING

"As a prisoner for the Lord, then, I urge you to live a life worthy of the calling you have received" (Ephesians 4:1).

Our prayers are answered not when we are given what we ask, but when we are challenged to be what we can be.
— Morris Adler

This section focuses on the calling stage of leadership. It addresses the time when the voice of the Lord says to a leader, "Come and follow me."

The key element of this calling stage is to hear the voice of the caller – and to discern it as God's. God calls people to where He wants them to be in order to complete His eternal purposes in and through them. His primary call is to a relationship with Him. The call to leadership, or to a particular kind of career or ministry, is completely secondary to that primary call to relationship.

How a person responds to God's call to relationship, then, will actually determine the depth and effectiveness of his or her leadership. Leadership is proven by reflecting the character of the ultimate leader, Jesus Christ, who defined His own leadership through service to others.

The outstanding qualifications of a leader are his or her willingness to follow the Lord Jesus Christ – and his or her willingness to believe the promises of God of whom is written, *"The one who calls you is faithful and he will do it,"* (1 Thessalonians 5:24).

The calling stage of the leadership journey includes:
- Hearing God
- Discerning God's voice
- Separating from the past
- Being set apart for God and His purposes
- Receiving and believing God's promises

Watch for these themes as you read chapters one and two.

Chapter 1

Discovering Your Call

The leadership journey begins with the call of God. But what does that call look like? How do you experience it? Those are questions that leaders have struggled with from biblical times to today.

One of my favorite accounts of God's calling on a life involves my friend Don Steiger. Don was my pastor for several years, but began his career with his sights set on becoming an electrical engineer. Quite a contrast, isn't it? And it was that very contrast that Don had to consider as he began his leadership journey. Not long ago, Don shared his story with me.

"I was privileged to grow up in a Christian home. My parents were sincere and godly examples to my brother, sister and me. They constantly exposed us to Christian training. We had devotions each morning, and they took us to church every time the doors were open.

"They created a very healthy spiritual environment. I came to faith in Jesus Christ as a child. As I grew older, my love for God increased. It only seemed right that I would pray for God to reveal His plan for my life – and I did that for some years as a young man.

"When I graduated from high school, I was determined to go to college. The challenge facing me was the same challenge facing any student: *What career path do I pursue?* The key for me as a Christian student was to try to figure out God's answer for that question.

"God's answer didn't come to me in blazing letters in the sky, by the way. It was a process of several years. I recall at the time I was finishing high school that an elder in our church asked if I would consider the ministry. I believe he saw God's hand on my life for pastoral ministry. I loved God and was very involved in the church, but my response to his question was, 'I would not do that unless God spoke to me clearly.'

"As I reflect on that now, after nearly three decades of pastoral ministry, I find that elder's insight still affirming. That being said, the insight of godly people can help affirm God's plan, but we still must discover it for ourselves – and at the time that elder asked me the question, I simply didn't sense a clear direction from God.

"Without clear direction from God, I looked at my aptitudes and the practical need to earn a living, and chose a career that I felt was honorable and profitable. I chose to study electrical engineering at the University of Colorado.

"I have no doubt God was in that decision, even though I did not have a sense of direction from Him at the time. I have come to realize that when God seems silent, we can trust our decisions if we are honestly seeking Him.

"One of the providential aspects of that decision was my introduction to my future wife. Figuring out God's will in this matter was easy. Two years before graduation I married Loretta Brown. She loved God with all her heart, but did not plan on being a pastor's wife.

"While we were dating, I drove her through a nice neighborhood and showed her the kind of house we would be able to afford when I finished my degree. I was building expectations based on my plans, as best I could figure them out. Even so, we wanted God's will above all else."

IS SOMEONE CALLING? IF SO, WHY?

Both Old and New Testament scriptures frequently mention the call of God. They show that the *purpose of God's calling is to draw people to where He wants them to be, in order to complete His eternal purposes in and through them.*

The call of God started in the Garden right after the Fall. (Remember Genesis 3:9: *But the LORD God called to the man, "Where are you?"*) The Lord Jesus started His ministry by calling individuals to the purposes of God. We hear the same calling by the Holy Spirit in the Book of Acts on the Day of Pentecost. And, as best we can tell, God's call will continue to draw people to where He wants them to be until the end of time.

There are two key considerations to consider in this calling stage of the journey:

- Hearing the voice of the caller, and
- Discerning that voice as being God's.

How does that happen? As we're about to find out, hearing and discerning God's voice is a process that pre-qualifies a person to be a Christian leader. Don's story demonstrates the process well.

First, *to hear God's voice, you have to listen.* And listening to God, like listening to a friend, requires that you put yourself in a position to listen. You focus your attention on God. You offer Him relevant conversation on the issues of your heart. You ask Him for guidance. You set apart time, and make the effort to seek Him out.

Second, *to discern God's voice, you need to know Him well.* It is one thing to ask God about an issue, and quite another to desire that you know Him better as a result of your encounter with Him.

Both of these elements make a healthy relationship with God crucial. These items also indicate that the seeker spend time in Bible study, in prayer, in fasting and in fellowship – just what we need to do to learn to hear and discern God's voice.

The reason Don's story demonstrates this process well is that he understood and owned his primary call to receive life through Jesus Christ, his ongoing responsibility to develop a relationship in Jesus Christ and his need to obediently serve Jesus Christ (whether he would become a pastor or an electrical engineer).

In these ways, God was already building Don to be a leader – just as He desires to build leadership qualities in each of us through His call. You see, God's call to every one of us involves three aspects:
- A call to life,
- A call to relationship, and
- A call to service.

No one who claims to be a Christian can escape the implications of God's calling. And what we do with each aspect determines our ability to be a godly leader – whether we're pastors of large churches or mechanics witnessing to our co-workers.

Let's take a deeper look at these aspects of God's calling.

THE CALL TO LIFE

God's desire for every person and nation is *salvation*. Therefore, the first aspect of God's call is a call to life. The Lord calls people to repentance. We are to come to Him for forgiveness of sin. This is His redemptive work.

This call is demonstrated to God's people throughout history. In fact, repentance was the main message of the Old Testament by the prophets to both the people of covenant and other nations. In the New Testament, the mission of local churches was to continue to voice that call as they declared the good news of salvation, calling people to the Lord. The focus of the Great Commission is the fulfillment of God's call to life: *the plan of salvation for all nations.*

Since the Day of Pentecost and throughout Church history, God the Holy Spirit has been calling all humanity to salvation by saying, *"The Spirit and the bride say, 'Come!' And let him who hears say, 'Come!' Whoever is thirsty, let him come; and whoever wishes, let him take the free gift of the water of life,"* (Rev. 22:17). This call will continue until the Lord Jesus comes back to fulfill His promise of the blessed hope for the saved.

The call of God to life is twofold. First, it is a call to become a child of God. John 1:12 says, *"Yet to all who received him, to those who believed in his name, he gave the right to become children of God...."* Second, it is a call to the fullness of life. Jesus said, *"The thief comes only is to steal and kill and destroy; I have come that they may have life, and have it to the full,"* (John 10:10).

Therefore the purpose of God's call to life is to bring us back to the original plan that God displayed in creation and fulfilled through His redemptive work in Christ. At creation God placed His own image, bestowed His likeness, and poured His blessings on humanity, just as the Bible says in Genesis 1:27-28: *"So God created man in his own image, in the image of God he created him; male and female he created them."* Further, the call to life is the entrance gate to blessings in Christ: *"Praise be to the God and Father of our Lord Jesus Christ, who has blessed us in the heavenly realms with every spiritual blessing in Christ,"* (Ephesians 1:3). God blesses us in all things because we belong to Christ.

Other calls God gives us are very much dependent on our response to the call to salvation and to the fullness of life in Christ Jesus. In fact, how a person responds to fullness in Christ Jesus determines the depth and effectiveness of his or her leadership call.

Responding fully to the call of salvation and blessings of God in Christ Jesus provides a solid foundation for the general and specific call of God on one's life.

Don Steiger's positive response to God's call to life through Jesus Christ provided such a foundation for his leadership journey.

CALL TO RELATIONSHIP

Responding to God's call to life establishes a lasting relationship with God. As Paul wrote the church in Ephesus, a person who responds to the call of life becomes a member of the family of God. Speaking to the Gentiles, He said: "*Consequently you are no longer foreigners and aliens* [strangers], *but fellow citizens with God's people and members of God's household* [family}," (Ephesians 2:19).

There is no stronger relationship than being a family member. That's why God calls us to Himself for a relationship before He calls us to ministry.

Jesus followed that same pattern, calling the Disciples to himself before He called them to ministry. In the Gospel of Mark we read, "*Jesus went up on a mountainside and called to him those he wanted, and they came to him. He appointed twelve - designating them apostles - that they might be with him and that he might send them out to preach…*" (Mark 3:13-14).

Let's review this pattern. In these verses we notice phrases such as "*called to him.*" They were called to a person, not to activities. "*They came to him*" means they established a relationship with Jesus before they went into ministry. To know Him, to love Him, to accept Him, to believe in Him, to fellowship with Him, to hear Him, to touch Him, to be touched and know they were formed by Him "…*that they might be with him.*" Again, this confirms that their primary call was to be with Jesus in relationship. In other words they were called *to* Him, but not based on what they could do *for* Him.

The temptation in our Christian walk, particularly for those in ministry, is to run *for* God before we learn to run *to* Him. It is more natural to do things in the name of the Lord than to establish a relationship with Him and worship Him. That is putting religion in the place of relationship.

The call to relationship has two aspects. The first concerns our relationship with God, while the second involves our relationship with others. God only works in the context of relationship. God is a God of relationship. He doesn't do anything outside of a relationship with Him and with others. The banks of God's river of blessings are our relationship with Him and our relationship with others. Whenever one of the banks is destroyed, the river becomes a flood. The flood is usually destructive. It is purposeless. It does not have a goal. This is why the Scriptures emphasize that we should love our God with our total being and love others as ourselves. Jesus said these are the first and second commandments.

A person who is serious about the call of God for his life can't afford to neglect his relationship with God and with his brothers and sisters in Christ. Keeping your relationships with God and others healthy is the best way to ensure success as a leader, wherever it is you exercise that role.

It isn't hard to notice that even as a young man Don Steiger's life was full of healthy relationships – with God, with his family, with those in church leadership and with his wife-to-be. It seems clear that Don knew how to respond well to this part of God's call.

CALL TO SERVICE

A call to ministry comes after the call to life, spiritual blessings and relationships with God and others. This is more than just a call to activities. This implies worship and commitment to doing His will.

King Hezekiah, who was a reformer during the restoration of the temple of God, reminded the priests of this truth by saying, *"My sons, do not be negligent now, for the LORD has chosen you to stand before him and serve him, to minister before* him and to burn incense," (2 Chronicles 29:11). In other words, responding to God's call to ministry is living a life worthy of the calling: to be a child of God and to have an ongoing relationship with Him.

What makes Christian ministry powerful is that it is a by-product of who we are as children of God. It is a result of our relationship with God through the indwelling of the Holy Spirit. Therefore, what is a Christian ministry?

When God calls us to serve Him, His call is not necessarily to "do" but to "be." From this perspective, *Christian ministry is total obedience to the revealed will of God.* As we pursue this ministry, we will reflect God's glory by modeling His character in love, holiness, purity and compassion. Our lives will show the active process of being changed into the likeness of Christ by the work of the Holy Spirit.

Again, this definition takes us out of the realm of activity into the realm of relationship. In so doing, it underscores the following points.

First, *the focus of Christian ministry is obedience rather than a particular activity.* God desires obedience from His children. Obeying His will means being a blessing and fulfilling His purpose, but not "being busy" for God. Activities can make a dedicated person religious, but they don't make him spiritual. Spirituality is a fruit of obedience to the will of God. That was the difference between the life and ministry of Jesus and the religious leaders of Jesus' time.

Second, *the crucial strategy in Christian ministry is the "revealed will of God," not what an individual thinks "looks good."* A person can be busy for God all his life without doing God's will. Paul highlighted the importance of this point by saying, "*And he made known to us the mystery of his will according to his good pleasure, which he purposed in Chris*t…" (Ephesians 1:9). It is an individual's responsibility to know the revealed will of God for his life and live it out.

Third, *the most important demonstration of Christian ministry is to reflect God's character.* Obeying God's revealed will wholeheartedly strengthens our relationship with Him and also builds His character in a person. Such maturity leads to *being* rather than *doing*. When ministry becomes a lifestyle, a person starts reflecting the character of Christ by "being."

Fourth, *what the Holy Spirit does in the life of a person is more important that what one does for God.* In fact, there is no spiritual ministry without a willingness to be transformed by the power of the Holy Spirit. God is more interested in what He can do in an individual than what He can do through them.

Fifth, *character building is more important than using spiritual gifts.* Character is the fruit of the Spirit. Ministry that doesn't produce the fruit of the Spirit depends too much on spiritual gifts alone. As good and important as they are, spiritual gifts don't substitute for quality of character and the fruits of the Spirit. Paul summarized this concept after he compared the Old and New Testament ministries by saying, *"And we, who with unveiled faces all reflect the Lord's glory, are being transformed into his likeness with ever-increasing glory, which comes from the Lord, who is the Spirit,"* (2 Corinthians 3:18). Such a process leads a person into being a true servant, just as Jesus was. Then ministry becomes the reflection of who a person is instead of the reflection of the people one is trying to serve.

It is indeed a process to perceive and receive God's calling at this level. We'll return to Don Steiger's story now to illustrate how he built on the calls of life and relationship to accept his call to serve.

ACCEPTING THE CALL

Don Steiger was anticipating a career as an electrical engineer, and all that went with it. He remained open to

God's call on his life, however, and that made all the difference.

As Don tells it, "Loretta, my wife, tells me that even when we were dating in college – and I was telling her about the life we could expect with a career as an electrical engineer – that she had an underlying sense we would end up in the ministry.

"Sure enough, during the two years leading up to graduation I experienced a growing desire to be involved in full-time ministry. I never heard a voice from heaven or received a vision, but the desires of my heart were changing. The thought of spending my days in the engineering profession left me feeling empty. On the other hand, when I would consider spending my time ministering the eternal things of God my heart would fill with meaning. I also noted that God blessed my work in the church and I began to recognize the spiritual gifts He had given me."

Just for a moment, let's stop to consider some nagging questions: *How do I know God is calling? How does He call? What method does He use?*

We must understand this simple truth: *The call of God is not uniform for every leader.* To some He speaks directly. He leads others through a process that will bring them to a place of submission to the divine calling.

The most important thing in a calling is to *understand* the call of God with clarity and *respond* to it with reverence and holy fear of the Lord. Isaiah was referring to this when he quoted God saying, *"This is the one I esteem: he who is humble and contrite in spirit, and trembles at my word,"* (Isaiah 66:2).

You'll notice that Don's experience of calling was not one dramatic event, but a process over years. Still, in time there was a defining moment of Don's call. As Don describes it, "I gradually became convinced that God was calling me to the ministry. I completed my degree and graduated with honors. Not knowing what to do, I decided to make myself available for ministry as I could, and delayed the start of my engineering career to see what God would do.

"My wife and I traveled to any church that would invite us to sing and speak. I continued to work at the job I held during college to make ends meet. Not long after, my home church called me to be an associate pastor. I regarded this as an answer to my prayerful search for God's direction and accepted the position."

Don's acceptance of God's call to ministry put him in the unique position to experience the *dimensions* of God's call. Before we continue Don's story, let's explore those dimensions.

Chapter 2

The Dimensions of God's Call

The call of God has three aspects or dimensions to it. One aspect is "call from." Dimension two is "called to" and dimension three is "called for."

Call from refers to the redemption process. God calls a person *from* sin to freedom. When God comes, He calls us *from* where we are to where we should be. In this sense, the initial call of God is calling individuals *from* the past of sins, failures, bondage, doubts, fears, darkness and insecurity into His ultimate purpose. Therefore it's *from*. God called the Israelites *from* bondage in Egypt. The primary call of God is *from*. Don Steiger experienced this dimension when he received Christ as his Savior, and each time he allowed God to move him into deeper maturity as a disciple and leader.

The second dimension of the call of God is *called to*. God doesn't only call from, but He *calls to* – *to* new things, new relationships, new hope, a new future, a life of forgiveness, a life of mercy, a life of freedom in Christ Jesus. God calls an individual *to* the life of God, the fullness of God and the blessings of God. This implies the total blessing of God for a person or child of God. Don experienced this dimension as he accepted each of God's blessings that resulted from his obedience.

A third dimension is *called for*. This is the call *for* the purpose of God. God calls people to His ultimate purpose. When He calls *from* to relationship, once a person leaves the past behind and comes to have the relationship with God, the call is a continuum into something God wants to accomplish through the person. In this sense: *called for* His purpose. A person is *called for* the purpose of God—to serve God, honor God, glorify God, worship God, walk with God and fulfill the ultimate plan of God. When we define a call God has *for* a person, *called for* is the result of calling *from* and *to*. This is fulfilling the purpose of God for an individual. It also reinforces a profound shift of expectations as leaders face changed circumstances that result from their pursuit of the calling. You'll see that this "continuum of calling" challenged Don in his early years of leadership as his story continues.

THE CALLING AND
THE CHALLENGE OF CIRCUMSTANCES

"The realities of being an associate pastor constantly challenged my ideas of what life as an electrical engineer might have been like. Instead of living in a nice house like I had shown Loretta two years earlier, we lived in a basement apartment in the church building. The beginning of this experience was exhilarating as I studied through a denominational 'distance learning' college. I also worked under the mentoring of a wonderful senior pastor.

"My calling, however, was challenged by circumstances about three years later. Our income was very small and my wife needed a new dress. I did not have enough money to buy her one. Seeing the need, her mother purchased a dress for her. We were both grateful, but inside I was embarrassed that I could not meet that need for my wife.

"I did not expect the ministry to be lucrative, but the reality of the sacrifice was hitting home. I went back to the university campus and signed up for job interviews in electrical engineering. I received a couple of offers and found myself wrestling with God's call on my life. I could not find peace with the idea of pursuing an engineering career.

"As my wife and I processed through this situation we both concluded that obeying God was worth whatever sacrifices we would have to make. I declined the opportunities and continued in the ministry.

"Six years into my work God spoke to me more clearly than ever before and told me it was time to leave that church. Without having anything else to go to, I resigned. I worked odd jobs for three months as I searched for a new pastoral position.

"It was then that God directed us to Colorado Springs and the church I would pastor for 22 years."

Do you see how Don had grown in his ability to face challenging circumstances? Take note of this: *The call of God is usually affirmed by His promises.* God reveals His purpose to individuals with promises. The promises God gives a leader are usually attainable by obeying His call. In other words, a person makes these promises a reality by accepting the will of God for his life.

Every leader needs a solid foundation to be effective. The promises of God provide that foundation, empowering the leader to stand firm during challenging times. Don was able to face a time when his future employment was uncertain because he understood that God's promises are His commitment to a leader, enabling the person to fulfill the call of leadership. The Bible tells us, *"For no matter how many promises God has made, they are 'Yes' in Christ. And so through him, the 'Amen' is spoken by us to the glory of God. Now it is God who makes both us and you stand firm in Christ. He anointed us..."* (2 Corinthians 1:20-21).

It is critical for a leader to understand the difference between personal desires and God's promises. A personal desire is a subject for prayer while the promises of God are God's commitment to equip a leader for ministry. Don didn't rely on his own desires as he sought guidance for the future when he left his first church. Instead, he believed in God's commitment to him as shown through God's promises.

This is a biblical pattern.

- **Abraham** operated in leadership based on God's promise of *blessing* to him: *"The LORD had said to Abram, 'Leave your country, your people and your father's household and go to the land I will show you. I will make you into a great nation and I will bless you; I will make your name great, and you will be a blessing. I will bless those who bless you, and whoever curses you I will curse; and all peoples on earth will be blessed through you,'"* (Genesis 12:1-3).

- **Joseph** became a leader through a promise given in a *dream*. (See Genesis 37:5-11 for a full account.) Joseph believed the dream God gave him and started living his life as a leader with integrity of character – despite the fact that God had not given Joseph a timetable, method or an idea of where he would exercise leadership.

- **Moses** followed God's call to leadership due to a *promise of protection in response to a special God-given burden*. God proved himself to Moses time and again with supernatural protection as Moses led Israel out of Egypt, through the wilderness and to the Promised Land. The proof of Moses' burden made history, as some 1300 years later the writer of Hebrews reminded the Early Church, *"By faith Moses, when he had grown up, refused to be known as the son of Pharaoh's daughter. He chose to be mistreated, along with the people of God, rather than to enjoy the pleasures of sin for a short time,"* (Hebrews 11:24-26).

- **Saul, David, and Elisha** all were promised power from on high through *anointing*. Their anointing was with oil, and in each case – at least for a time – these leaders operated in the power and promises of God. *Jesus* set the best example of leadership in the anointing of the Holy Spirit and power, as Peter testified in Acts 10:38: *"...how God anointed Jesus of Nazareth with the Holy Spirit and power, and how he went around doing good and healing all who were under the power of the devil, because God was with him."*

- **Jeremiah** was blessed with the promise of God's *touch* on his life. This divine touch is common in each call God issues to leaders. After God touched Jeremiah, the prophet became assured of God's presence with him. That touch also brought power, strength, knowledge, wisdom and much more. (See Jeremiah 1:10.)
- **Jesus' disciples** exercised leadership as they believed in the promise of His *direction*. The disciples were true adventurers. They accepted Jesus' call to follow Him without a detailed roadmap. They simply had the willingness to drop what they were doing and follow the true leader, the Lord Jesus Christ. (See Matthew 4:19.)
- **Paul** followed the promise of a clear *vision* in his ministry. It allowed the Apostle to say in a difficult time, *"So then...I was not disobedient to the vision from heaven,"* (Acts 26:19). It is striking that the same vision of Jesus that blinded Paul for a time became the guidepost for his leadership journey!

LESSONS LEARNED

Don learned a lot as he dealt with God's calling on his life. He explains, "Discerning the call of God in my life was a process. Looking back I can see the factors that insured the discovery of his plan for me.

"First of all, I needed to maintain my personal relationship with Jesus Christ and keep growing in Him. The principal calling of God is universal, and that is to know Him and become like Him. Second, I needed to actively wait on God and apply myself to what was at hand. I worked at developing a future with the wisdom and opportunities available. I stayed active in service for Christ, doing whatever I could in the church, developing a servant's heart and discovering the spiritual gifts God had placed in my life.

"Third, I needed to listen to trustworthy people God had placed in my life. Fourth, I needed to trust the providence of God. I had to believe God was guiding me even when I had to make decisions without knowing for sure what God wanted me to do. Fifth, the desires of my heart became a source of understanding God's will as I continued to seek Him. Also, I found that I experienced peace in my heart when I was doing what God wanted, even if it entailed trials or sacrifice. Sixth, I needed to be ready to obey when God gave direction to me, even though it might involve risk, and again, sacrifice."

SO WHERE CAN YOU GO FROM HERE?

You may be working through the process – and remember, it *is* a process – of discovering God's calling for your life. If you believe God is calling you to serve Him in some specific way, it could be tempting to attach God's primary call to that task. But remember that God's primary call is to a *relationship*.

With that in mind, you're ready to do what it takes to *hear God's voice*, and to know Him well enough to *determine that voice is His*. Keep praying and fasting. Study the Word. Stay in fellowship. Ask God to lead you specifically into His calling for you.

The calling stage also involves *separation from the past*. For Moses, it meant he could no longer hide in Midian as a shepherd – he had to become a leader. For Don Steiger, it meant giving up the idea of electrical engineering as a profession. Your past hurts, your former expectations, your previous failures and successes are behind you. As you work through the calling stage, you will learn to rejoice in the truth that today and the future are God's.

For a leader, the calling stage is also a time to be *set apart for God and His purposes*. Sometimes your leadership calling will be recognized by others before you even recognize it. Don's elder in his home church had that sort of insight. In the Bible, you'll recall that Samuel knew David would be king of Israel long before David understood the implications of that role.

Finally, the calling stage is your introduction to *receiving God's promises*. Vision, blessings, direction, dreams and daily bread are all part of God's commitment to you. Seek out God, ask for them and receive them with joy.

One last note: *The calling stage is often applied to younger people.* To be sure, Bible characters like Jeremiah, Mary, Daniel and Samuel (and modern leaders like Don Steiger) started working through their calls as young people. But Noah, Moses and many pastors and teachers I know were just working through this stage as adults – some middle-aged, others into their golden years. *Age is no limit in the economy of God's kingdom.*

Let God use His calling for your life to start you on the journey that will complete His eternal purposes in, through and for you.

QUESTIONS FOR REFLECTION

1. *What are the possible dangers of comparing your experience of God's calling to that of others? Could there be any advantages to such comparison?*
2. *What promises of God do you see active in your life as you pursue His calling?*

How might you explain God's calling to someone else who could be struggling with the issue?

Stage 2
The Leadership Journey

I The Call
Process of >Hearing >Discerning >Promise >From, to and for

II Acceptance
Process of >Step of faith >Entering >Commission >Confirmation >Signs

III Early Leadership
Process of >History >Ministry >People >Team

IV Reality
Process of >Character building >Self discovery >Facing reality >Personal gifts >Call >God >Knowledge

V Maturity
Process of >Building Ministry >Recognizing offices >Correcting History >Making History >Shaping History

VI Value Stage
Process of >Relationship >Building people >Becoming a father >Bearing Fruit >Establishing Pattern

VII Relational Stage
Process of >Relationship >Leaving a legacy

II Acceptance
Process of
>Step of faith
>Entering
>Commission
>Confirmation
>Signs

ACCEPTING THE CALL

"My Presence will go with you, and I will give you rest"
(Exodus 33:14)

'Tis not the dying for a faith that's so hard;
'tis the living up to it that is difficult.
— William Makepeace Thackeray

The spiritual leader is called to advance God's kingdom by carrying out God's agenda. Accepting God's call, then, involves discerning and obeying that agenda.

Some of the questions that come with this stage in the leadership journey include, *Who are you, Lord?* and *What would you have me do?*

The answers become clearer as a leader moves out in faith. That obedience results in God's assurance that He is with the leader, and has indeed commissioned the leader. The leader discovers that the call of the leader is always to bring about the purposes of God for His people.

God's agenda of service, then, implies building a bridge between God and His people. It is the call of a leader to be involved in the repairing and rebuilding of broken lives, families, societies, churches, communities and organizations. Accepting God's call often means taking on a career in something that is not "professional church work." Yet the leader is able to continue on the journey, regardless of the profession it entails, with the strength found only in God and His promises. The leader takes special solace in God's promise of direction at this stage: *"My Presence will go with you, and I will give you rest,"* (Exodus 33:14). This part of the leadership journey includes:

- Taking steps of faith
- Being commissioned
- Receiving confirmation
- Accepting God's will
- Following divine signs
- Commitment to the calling

Watch for these steps in the process of accepting the call as you read chapters three and four.

Chapter 3

Receiving the Pass

Imagine the last minute of an exciting soccer match. The score is tied. Your team is driving toward the opponent's goal. You've taken a wing position on the field, joining your team on the drive. The center sees an opening in front of you and skillfully passes the ball in your direction.

Do you stop running toward the ball at that moment? Do you turn in the other direction, humbly saying, "No, no. It's not my place to kick the winning goal."

Let's hope not, for the sake of your team. At the same time, let's be honest: Many of us are tempted to treat God's call on our lives in the same way. Having seen the way to His goal for our lives, God delivers His call to us – and it can be incredibly easy to back away from that call.

God gives the call. We have to receive it.

Almost every leader I know has struggled with this issue. David Burdine, a successful accountant who heads up Bethesda Ministries, is truly transparent about his own experience in accepting God's call.

"I'm a lay person. Talking about the 'call of God' can be intimidating for us. We almost have a guilt trip about the call of God. We think everyone in ministry has heard a deep, booming voice saying, 'Hey, you! Here's your calling!' Our challenge is to remember that God's calling extends to every career, every kind of service.

"That was the big challenge for me. I lived with a sense of inadequacy for many years wondering, 'Why did God call all these preachers and not *me*?' But God *had* called me.

"Perhaps part of my struggle was that I didn't see myself as a likely candidate for God's calling. I came from a broken home. My mother and father divorced early in my life. In fact, I never saw my father more than once or twice after the divorce. Mom overcompensated for being a divorcee in a time when it wasn't socially acceptable by going overboard with 'dos' and 'don'ts'. I'm sure Mom protected me from many things with that approach. Yet it made me even more determined to chart my own course in college.

"*Charting my own course* didn't involve running away from God. I was blessed with a firm grip on my relationship with Jesus Christ at a young age. What it *did* mean was that I was actively seeking to make my life count. Early in my college days, a line from an old song burned its way into my heart:

If I can help somebody while I pass this way,
Then my living shall not be in vain.

"Over the years, I've come to believe that God speaks to us through songs. I took these words very seriously. I was pursuing a degree in accounting. I had no inclination for what I perceived to be professional ministry. I realized I wanted to be involved in business and to see people's quality of life improved through my work.

"What I knew without a doubt was something confirmed through my wife Sharon when we were married. We decided that we would attempt to fling the net of God's love over as many lost and hurting people as we could. We had no idea what that would mean, but that decision was at the heart of how we pursued our life together."

GOD'S AGENDA

The focus of this stage in the leadership journey is to understand God's purposes so you can commit fully to them. You can see in David Burdine's story that his commitment to God's purposes – *even in a role outside of traditional 'ministry' leadership* – defines his life as that of a Christian leader.

For a time, David thought that God wouldn't call him because he wasn't pursuing a profession traditionally associated with God's calling. But that wasn't the case. You see, the *profession* of a leader is never as important as his or her commitment to God's *purpose* for their life.

There are some common identifiable responsibilities of God's calling for people who are called to leadership positions. The first one is to *show God*.

Every leader should respond to a request like that Philip made of Jesus: "*Lord, show us the Father and that will be enough for us,*" (John 14:8).

A characteristic of a spiritual leader is to show the Father. That means a leader must reflect the character of God in all areas. The leader's followers expect this, as does God. What makes a lasting, positive impact on others is what they see in the life of a leader. Spiritual leaders provide direction – direction toward their Creator, Redeemer, Healer, Provider and Keeper. A leader maximizes his effectiveness by connecting to God, the greatest resource for every need.

The second responsibility in the life of a leader is to *carry out the purpose of God*. In every generation, God looks for people who will serve His purpose. The Bible sums up the life history of King David of Israel in one short statement by saying, "*For when David had served God's purpose in his own generation, he fell asleep....*" (Acts 13:36).

That description of King David is crucial. It indicates that to carry out God's purpose successfully, a leader must understand two things:

- First, God's purpose; and
- Second, our own generation.

Let's consider those two issues now.

God's purpose is the fullness He intended for His creation. Jesus said as much when He described His mission as the Good Shepherd: *"I have come that they may have life, and have it to the full,"* (John 10:10b). So what makes up the "fullness" God intends for us? At the very least, it includes salvation, peace, joy, health, blessings, spiritual gifts and spiritual well-being.

How does God's purpose work out in a leader's specific situation? How can a leader know it? There is a lifetime of "curriculum" that leaders must continually review:

1) *The overall plan of God* in creation and redemption.
2) *The core message of the Bible* as being the heart of God; the Father's purpose revealed in a heart of compassion and mercy.
3) *The mind of Christ.* We are told we have the mind of Christ in 1 Corinthians 2:16. The characteristics of the mind of Christ are revealed in Philippians 2, and include love, unselfishness and humility.
4) *The power of the revelation of the Holy Spirit.* God the Father made known His plan because of His love and mercy. God the Son made it possible for the plan of God to become a reality by His death and resurrection. God the Holy Spirit reveals the plan and purpose of God and empowers those who are committed to fulfill His purpose.
5) *Kingdom purpose, character and principles.* God does everything in the context of His kingdom. The primary responsibility of a spiritual leader is to advance the kingdom of God by carrying out Kingdom agenda. Lack of understanding of the purpose of God leads a leader to build a personal kingdom at the expense of God's kingdom. There is only one Kingdom to build and one King to serve in this life.

6) *Divine revelation.* It is impossible to know the purpose of God without the revelation God gives by the anointing of the Holy Spirit. Such revelation is the result of having relationship with God through repentance and forgiveness of sin. The Lord Jesus gives this to those who trust in Him as personal Savior and Lord. That is why for a leader, serving God's purpose is more than having leadership and/or management skills.

What does that purpose look like in a leader's specific situation? God's purpose will remain the same, but circumstances may demand a different exterior. For example, "life to the full" might mean helping the poor do better economically for a leader in a developing country. In contrast, in a developed nation a leader might need to show others how to divest themselves of needless possessions to enjoy "life to the full."

It comes down to serving God's purpose in your own generation. This requires knowing the generation – its needs, challenges, fears, hopes, problems, character and successes.

A leader is to be a bridge between the purpose of God and the generation. God looks to every generation for an individual who will stand in the gap before the Lord. This leader brings together the holy purpose of God and the generation that needs the Lord's mercy. This is what King David, who had a heart after God, did. He served the Lord's purpose in his own generation.

David was able to bridge the gap between God's plan for his people and their situation. David, through worship and commitment to seeking the Lord and obeying Him, brought back the centrality of God to every aspect in their activities of life. His songs of prayers also reflected his desire to bring together the purpose of God and the coming generation when he said, *"Since my youth, O God, you have taught me, and to this day I declare your marvelous deeds. Even when I am old and gray, do not forsake me, O God, till I declare your power to the next generation, your might to all who are to come,"* (Psalm 71:17-18).

Someone is positioned for leadership when he understands God's purpose and his own generation. God's agenda is formed when a leader determines to be a bridge between the two.

Back to the other David (Burdine) in this chapter. Notice how David, in harmony with his wife Sharon, agreed to be a bridge between God's purpose and his own generation: "We decided that we would attempt to fling the net of God's love over as many lost and hurting people as we could."

David Burdine determined to take God's purpose to a generation of people who needed it. That simple commitment positioned David perfectly for leadership, even when he wasn't seeking it. Let's continue with his story.

THE MILLION DOLLAR PASSION

"I have always been a goal setter. I think many of us miss out on what God would have us do because we don't take the opportunity to prayerfully put our commitments on paper.

"One of the earliest things I put on paper as a goal – maybe a dream – was to be in a position to give away a million dollars a year. My friends thought it was silly. Sharon didn't. But that piece of paper was something I kept in my desk wherever I worked through the early years.

"I believe part of God's call is going with what you like to do. Before I declared a major in college, I took an accounting course. My test scores surprised the professor. They were a shock to me, too. He called me aside toward the end of the course and said, 'You've tested really high all semester. Do you want to be an accounting major?'

"It's a great blessing to be able to do something you like. I loved being an accounting major, and when I graduated, I loved being an accountant. My first position was with Bethesda Care Centers, which was then engaged in the nursing home and hospital business. I began a seven-year stint as an accountant when I graduated from college. I was happy in that position.

"I believed I was the shyest kid in the world, and that belief carried with me into my teen years. I was so shy I never even went to a church youth camp. I lived at home all four years of college. But there was a fire building in me – God was nurturing a great passion in my soul.

"Sharon helped me put it into words: 'casting the net of God's love over as many lost and hurting people as we could.' I still didn't know how it would happen, but I began to believe God would someday do something with that passion. Because I was an introvert, however, I had no inkling that it might involve a leadership position.

"After seven years with Bethesda, I took an accounting position for a construction firm. I left Bethesda on the best of terms. It just seemed that it was time to leave.

"We loved our new location in San Jose, California. We loved our church situation. We made a comfortable living that allowed us to invest in God's kingdom, although it wasn't to the tune of a million dollars a year – we were able to give a few tens of thousands.

"But that burning in my soul never left. If anything, it grew – and I had no idea what to do with it.

"I was as surprised as anyone when the Bethesda Board of Directors offered me the presidency of Bethesda. I kept them at bay for a year. I wasn't brilliant, but I did have common sense. My resume didn't shout 'leader,' but I did have a passion – and that passion ended up being the defining reason I finally took the job.

"I was concerned about going into an insecure situation. Bethesda owned about 15 nursing homes and two acute care hospitals, and was in serious jeopardy of going bankrupt after losing more than three million dollars.

"But even with all that staring me in the face, I believed Bethesda might become the vehicle for that dream to become a reality. I sensed that somehow God might satisfy the passion He placed within me as I took on that challenge.

"The key question for me was one of being available. It was one of saying 'yes' to a difficult situation in the belief that God knew what He was doing, even when I didn't have a blueprint of His will in front of me."

David Burdine's example proves the Kingdom value of "receiving the pass." Receiving God's call indeed makes all the difference in the life of a leader. But the journey goes on. We must meet the challenges of the Call in God's timing and strength.

Chapter 4
Accepting the Challenge

We dare not minimize the challenges of accepting God's call. To accept something means to submit or say "yes" to it. It is to say, "Okay, Lord."

Earlier we discussed the call of God. Once a person understands the call or purpose of God for his or her life, then in the acceptance stage the individual submits to it. Accepting God's call is, in this sense, a commitment to obey the revealed will and purpose of God for one's life.

At this stage, the most crucial thing is that God affirms it through His presence. At the calling stage, the crucial thing God gives His people is His promises. In the acceptance stage, it's the manifestation of His presence. As we accept the presence of God, it becomes a positive sign to us.

Again, God's presence is a positive sign that God gives His children to confirm His will. But a number of people never get that far in the leadership journey. Instead, they fall prey to one of the challenges that face them in accepting the call. Let's look at some of those challenges now.

1. FEAR OF FAILURE

The first challenge is the fear of failure. It's that sinking feeling that comes with the question, "What happens if I'm not able to do it?"

This challenge is due to the wrong focus. Here, the potential leader doesn't see God, who is calling him or her. Rather, the person has a tendency to look at what he or she *has*. The result is a continual comparison between *our resources* and *God's mission*. We stack up what we think we have – a gift, a certain ability or whatever we believe is important for the calling – against the magnitude of what God has called us to do. Then we are apt to say, "No. If I accept this I will fail. I can't do this, so I won't try."

We see these struggles in the life of Moses. Moses recognized the greatness of God and the power of God. But the challenge came when the Lord asked him to go to Pharaoh and tell him to set the people of God free. Moses assessed his lack of skills against this enormous task, and at first completely forgot to factor God's power into the situation. The result was an overwhelming fear of failure: "No Lord, how can I do this? Pharaoh won't listen to me. Besides, what will happen if I do this? No matter what I do, Pharaoh will still refuse to free your people. I'll look like a fool. He might even throw me in prison."

When Moses let his personal reputation become the issue, fear of failure became the inevitable result. It's a constant challenge throughout a leader's life.

2. FEELINGS OF INADEQUACY

The second challenge in accepting the call is the feeling of inadequacy. This is clearly related to the fear of failure, but focuses less on one's reputation and more on the enormity of what God's purpose for a leader is.

The prophet Jeremiah clearly demonstrated this issue. When the Lord spoke to Jeremiah, called him, and revealed His purpose to him, Jeremiah struggled with feelings of inadequacy. He said, "Lord, I'm just a child. I can't do this." He was referring to his age, lack of experience and maybe even lack of knowledge that he believed would be necessary to carry out what God was asking him to do. Jeremiah's initial response to God's calling was to remind God that he was just a child.

David Burdine's story also reflects this challenge in the early days. David's feeling of inadequacy showed as he struggled with his perceived lack of talent for anything having to do with ministry. He felt he had no known talent or special ability that he believed went along with the calling of God.

The manifestation of inadequacy always comes when we say, "I am just . . ." That means something is lacking, to be sure. But what is lacking is not a particular gift or talent. Rather, what is lacking is the focus needed to deal with God's calling: not a focus on our own inadequacies, but a focus on the enabling power, presence and promises of God.

You may have already sensed that David Burdine found the proper focus and, with God's blessing, made the most of it. We'll go back to his story in a short while. For now, we need to consider a few other challenges in accepting God's call.

3. UNCERTAINTY

Uncertainty is the third challenge a leader faces in accepting the call of God. You can understand the call of God. You can hear it and take a step of faith in response to it – yet still be uncertain about it.

Gideon, a judge of Israel, went through exactly that experience. God had called Gideon to defeat the great army of Midianites who had been ravaging Israel for seven years. Gideon was uncertain about God's calling for him, so every step along the way he asked God for a sign to confirm his calling to the task. God did not deny Gideon those signs, but it was as though Gideon had not heard from the beginning:

"*The LORD is with you, mighty warrior…Go in the strength you have and save Israel out of Midian's hand. Am I not sending you?… I will be with you, and you will strike down all the Midianites together,*" (Judges 6:12, 14, 16).

We should not become too harsh in our judgment of Gideon. Once a person understands, hears or receives the call of God, accepts and takes a step of faith, the challenge of being unsure comes. Even when a person hears clearly from the Lord, in taking the first step the person begins to doubt. He begins to wonder if the Lord really called him. *Are these just my feelings?* he might wonder. This particularly happens when the call is challenging and something the person is unfamiliar with – as with Gideon facing the call to lead Israel against the Midianites.

If the call is in line with something we expect or desire, then the uncertainty isn't as great or challenging. But when God says, "Change your ways. Think differently. This is what I want you to do," and it's not what we expected, is it any wonder that fear, doubt and uncertainty settle in? This is the biggest challenge a leader struggles with in this stage. *"God, is this really you? Is what I heard truly from you?"*

4. FEAR OF PAYING THE PRICE

The fourth challenge in accepting God's call is the fear of paying the price for the calling. The call of God comes with a price tag. The price tag varies according to the calling, God's purpose, what God wants to accomplish and what He wants to accomplish in a person.

In this stage individuals who want to accept the calling have a tendency to compare themselves with others. That was the case with Peter as Jesus challenged him to take on God's calling for his life. Jesus pointed out that Peter would pay a price to carry out the call of God to "feed his sheep" as a leader:

> *"...I tell you the truth, when you were younger you dressed yourself and went where you wanted; but when you are old you will stretch out your hands, and someone else will dress you and lead you where you do not want to go." Jesus said this to indicate the kind of death by which Peter would glorify God. Then he said to him, "Follow me!"*
>
> *Peter turned and saw that the disciple whom Jesus loved was following them. (This was the one who had leaned back against Jesus at the supper and had said, "Lord, who is going to betray you?") When Peter saw him, he asked, "Lord, what about him?"*
>
> *Jesus answered, "If I want him to remain alive until I return, what is that to you? You must follow me,"* (John 21:18-21).

The challenge is to be willing to pay the price. You may have to leave behind that which is familiar, as did Abraham. You might have to sacrifice comfort, as did Moses.

Even Jesus had to pay the price when He accepted the call of his Father. In Philippians chapter 2, we read of the price Jesus paid for accepting the calling. Initially when He came, the Bible tells us how much He humbled himself, *"...Who, being in very nature God, did not consider equality with God something to be grasped,"* (Philippians 2:6).

In other words, from an eternity of being equal with God, Jesus left that honor and humbled himself. He emptied himself, and took the very nature of a servant, being made in human likeness. His price? Exchanging equality with God for limiting himself to the flesh in an obscure place. This was the Creator of the universe, the One who spoke a word and everything came into existence. He created gold, silver and all resources. But He did not have a place to lie down when He was on earth. That was the material price Jesus paid in humbling himself.

There was even a greater price as Jesus obeyed the Father and went to the Cross: the price of being humiliated by the people He created! Jesus endured torture, humiliation, crucifixion and burial. Even His Father turned His face from Him, because of our sins. He had to cry like a created being, *"My Father, my Father, why have you forsaken me?"* The price of death was the price of accomplishing God's will, saying to the Father, *"It's not my will but your will."*

Limiting himself was the price Jesus paid. The price Jesus paid should remind us all that the call of God is not free. The true calling of God costs us something.

5. NEED FOR FURTHER CONFIRMATION

The fifth challenge in accepting God's calling is searching for confirmation. We saw this in action through Gideon's uncertainty in the example above. Let's explore this issue further through the example of Moses.

For Gideon, the need for confirming signs surrounded one situation: the battle against the Midianites. At most, his challenge with uncertainty lasted for a few months. For Moses, the need for signs early in his leadership journey was not used as a confirmation of God's calling, but rather as a challenge to God's wisdom. Moses seems to say to God after each sign, "Here. See how powerful you are? Then how wise can you be to use me to lead your people?"

Call it fear, arrogance or doubt on Moses' part. But instead of obeying and running with the will of God in his calling, Moses launched into a perpetual search for additional confirmation and more signs early in his role as a leader. Moses asked God, "When the Pharaoh asks me how I know it's you telling me to lead Israel, what do I tell him?" God responded by directing Moses to throw his walking stick to the ground. When Moses complied, the stick became a snake. Then God told him to pick it up. He did, and still he wasn't satisfied. Then God performed a second miracle. The Lord said, "Put your hand inside your cloak." Moses put his hand in his cloak, and when he took it out, it was leprous like snow. The Lord told him to put it back, and he did. When Moses took it out again the second time, his hand was restored.

That could have been enough to convince Moses, but somehow it wasn't. He still wanted more confirmation. The Lord then performed a third miracle for him. "If they don't believe you or pay attention to the first miracle or sign, they may believe the second. But if they don't believe these two signs, or listen to you, take some water from the Nile and throw it on dry ground. The water you take from the river will become blood on the ground." God performed this third miracle – and still Moses asked for more confirmation.

The temptation at this level is that a person tries to lead without faith. He or she seeks signs rather than God's will. This kind of leader wants an answer to every question. In this case, there are not enough miracles. After one miracle, a person wants still another confirmation, then another miracle or sign, and other wonders. Instead of coming back and saying, "Yes Lord, the positive sign you've given me is a confirmation of your presence and I'll act upon this," they continue to look for more signs of confirmation. That's the big challenge.

In Moses' case, even after the third miracle, he reasoned and said, "You've given me three confirmations or positive signs, but Lord, I'm really not the right person." Why? "Oh Lord, I've never been eloquent, neither in the past, nor since you've spoken to your servant. I'm slow of speech and tongue."

What is Moses doing? He's still saying, "Yes, I saw the miracles, but I still have questions." What a person needs to realize is this: *The miracles and signs God offers to a leader are given at this stage to help him take a step of faith –* **not** *to solve every problem a person might sense, see or fear.*

6. DESIRE TO UNDERSTAND BEFOREHAND

The sixth challenge of the acceptance stage is that a person tries to find a complete answer to the question "What does this mean?" far too early in the leadership journey – a desire to understand beforehand.

It could have been tempting for Joshua to ask God the meaning behind his call to step into the Jordan River. God had stated it plainly: "*Now then, you and all these people, get ready to cross the Jordan River into the land I am about to give to them – to the Israelites,*" (Joshua 1:2). God gave more detailed instructions a bit later: "*Today I will begin to exalt you in the eyes of all Israel, so they may know I am with you as I was with Moses. Tell the priests who carry the Ark of the Covenant: 'When you reach the edge of the Jordan's waters, go and stand in the river,'*" (Joshua 3:7, 8).

For the Israelites, Joshua could have said, "God, are you telling us to cross the Jordan? That's fantastic! But Lord, instead of asking us to put our feet into the water, why don't you divide it for us? What's the meaning of getting ready and putting our feet into the water? Why do we have to carry the Ark of the Covenant? Why do the priests have to go before the people and put their feet into the water? What is the meaning of this?"

God doesn't work that way. We can ask and ask, but the purpose of God is for us to take a step of faith. *Then*, in His time, God offers the meaning behind it. In Joshua's case, God might have responded, "I'm asking the priests to carry the Ark of the Covenant and step into the river because of my promises and assurance to my people that, through the Ark of the Covenant my presence is there. Where my presence is, nothing will stop you from entering into what I have for you. Nothing will stop you from possessing the land I have promised your fathers."

You can't find out the meaning behind God's call and direction by standing at the riverside and asking questions. Accepting the call means stepping out in faith.

7. WANTING TO HAVE A ROADMAP BEFOREHAND

It can be tempting for a leader to say, "Lord, I like what you're saying. I'm willing to go where you want me to go, accept the calling and even pay the price. I'm even willing to trust you for my inadequacies. Lord, I'm willing to trust your Word for unanswered questions, but please give me a road map. Draw a map for me – where I am to start, where I should go and where I will end up."

The desire for a road map is the seventh challenge in accepting God's call. We human beings like to have the road mapped out and everything in place before we accept the calling. The challenge, of course, is that God doesn't work that way. Consider the experience of Saul, the persecutor of the Church, as he was about to be transformed into Paul, the apostle of Jesus Christ:

> *As he* [Saul] *neared Damascus on his journey, suddenly a light from heaven flashed around him. He fell to the ground and heard a voice say to him, "Saul, Saul, why do you persecute me?"*
> *"Who are you, Lord?" Saul asked.*
> *"I am Jesus, whom you are persecuting,"* he replied. *"Now get up and go into the city, and you will be told what you must do,"* (Acts 9:3-6).

When God revealed himself to Paul and called him, Paul saw the light in midday, and heard the voice. He simply asked, "Lord, who are you?" He didn't ask for details, a game plan, an itinerary or a road map. He was ready to comply when the Lord Jesus directed him to go into Damascus and wait to be told the next step in his journey.

If you're looking for a road map, you might miss the light God has for your next step. Leadership is a step-by-step process because God reveals things one step at a time.

8. DESIRE TO HAVE ASSURANCE OF SUCCESS

The eighth challenge in accepting God's calling is the desire to have assurance of success before we start.

Leaders are not immune to the desire for success. In fact, leaders *must* have a desire for the success of God's work. But can we be assured of success before we begin?

Once again, God doesn't work this way. Ministry is not only what God uses a person to do in the lives of others or for His kingdom, but ministry is also what God does in the life of the individual whom He calls. It's the shaping, molding, changing and character building that takes place within us. That "molding" is part of the call to the ministry, too. God uses that process to develop us and bring us into the likeness of Jesus Christ.

That's why Jesus said, "Follow me and I will *make* you fishers of men." It's the *making*. It isn't only anointing, using and sending individuals out. It's the making, shaping and molding that also takes place in their lives. So be aware of this: God does not give assurance of success in the *human* measurement of success. When a person is in the will of God, everything a person does is successful. But it's not evaluated by human measurement. Success or failure is a matter of whether or not we're in the center of the will of God. When we're not in the center of God's will, we fail. When we're in the center of God's will and totally obey the revealed will of God for our personal life, we *are*, according to God, very successful people.

We should note here that not every person faces all of the challenges listed above. David Burdine, for example, struggled with his own feelings of inadequacy, but he was more than willing to pay the price to follow God's will. As his story continues, you'll discover David is, in fact, a profound example of someone who obeyed God one step at a time. He demonstrated no real desire for a roadmap or guarantees for success in human terms that others of us might struggle with.

Let's return now to David's story as he works through what it means to accept God's calling.

IT'S NOT HOW GREAT, BUT HOW AVAILABLE YOU ARE

David says, "As I was taking the helm at Bethesda, a friend challenged me with these words: 'Dave, don't try to prove to God how great you are, just prove how available you are.'

"That proved to be the key for me in accepting and working out God's call in my life. I couldn't pretend to be a great leader in the business world. My resume didn't support that. But I could be available to what God wanted to do with me.

"The road at Bethesda began with some tough decisions. I had to immediately deal with one hospital in Lincoln, Nebraska, that was losing hundreds of thousands of dollars each year. I made a proposal to the Lincoln City Council one wintry January night that would have solved some big issues for us. Remember, we were $3 million in the red, and had hundreds of thousands of dollars in past due bills.

"But the Council denied my request and I was devastated. There I was, president of Bethesda for four short months with one great idea to turn the ship around – and I'd been shot down. I fought a blizzard that was blowing in just to get to my car after the meeting. The roads were covered with ice, the storm was getting worse by the minute and I felt like a complete failure.

"I was desperate. I didn't just cry out to God; I was sobbing like a baby before God. The only word that came out of my mouth for the first few minutes on that drive home was 'Why?'

"And almost as soon as I voiced that question, I sensed a sudden divine Presence in the car with me. To my surprise, I started singing. It was a chorus I'd grown up with:

> *Far away in the depths of my spirit tonight,*
> *Lies a melody sweeter than psalm,*
> *In celestial-like strains, it unceasingly falls*

Stage 2: Accepting the Call

> *O'er my soul like an infinite calm.*
> *Peace, peace, wonderful peace*
> *Coming down from the Father above*
> *Sweep over my spirit forever I pray,*
> *In fathomless billows of love.*

"My tears were gone. My disappointment disappeared. The sense of devastation vanished. I had peace in my soul. God was confirming that His will was being done.

"I had a passion for missions and I knew of a missionary in India named Mark Buntain who was working among the poorest of the poor in Calcutta. I knew Rev. Buntain was trying to establish and equip a hospital there. My great idea had gone nowhere with the Lincoln City Council. The least I could do was to see what God might do if I made something out of the situation available for the Kingdom.

"Not too much later, I was on the phone with Mark Buntain. I said, 'Pastor Buntain, we have a hospital we are closing. It's full of old equipment. We'll give you any of it you like, if you can use it for your new hospital. The one catch is we can't afford to ship it or pay any duty to get it past customs for you.'

"That was a huge challenge. India was trying to assert its ability to stand on its own at the time, so any equipment coming in – even charitably given – was being assessed for duty at 100 percent of its new value.

"Mark wasn't put off by the situation. He said, 'You might have some equipment I haven't been able to find. It just happens that I'm leaving for America this Tuesday to take care of some details for opening the hospital in April.' And on the following Saturday, Mark and I were on the fourth floor of the Bethesda Hospital in Lincoln, Nebraska. That floor held our operating rooms.

"If Bethesda Hospital in Lincoln had a specialty, it was orthopedics. The first operating room we visited had a mobile orthopedic operating table that was unique. Mark instantly recognized it as something he'd been searching for. He selected that table, our anesthesia machines, our traction equipment and some surgical tools – all in all, about $5,000 worth of gear on the used hospital equipment market. The problem was, it would probably cost many times more to get the equipment in place in Calcutta.

"One week later, Mark called with the news that a moving company owner had offered to pick up the equipment in Nebraska and ship it to Calcutta – free of charge! And Mark had only mentioned that we'd donated the equipment. He'd said nothing about the need for shipping.

"Mark returned to India, still facing the duty issue. He told the story of the donated equipment and shipping to the import office in Calcutta. They volunteered that if Rev. Buntain would also do research at the hospital, they would issue an import license that would allow the equipment into the country duty free. That day, the hospital added research to its list of services rendered.

"The leadership of Bethesda – from the board to yours truly, its new president – was so taken by what God could do with what we made available that we pledged to share our income. We made that pledge and kept to it while we were still in the red. But the fun was just beginning.

"We finally sold that hospital in Lincoln a few months later. That was one-third of a million dollars lifted off our backs annually. Just three years later, Bethesda was running at a profit again.

"But I am living testimony to the fact that my leading Bethesda out of the red had nothing to do with a great idea. It had everything to do with availability."

THE MILLION DOLLAR VISION REVISITED – AND EXPANDED

"Over 24 years ago, when I became president of Bethesda, I thought I was a big dreamer. I had a long-standing goal to give $1 million annually to the work of the Kingdom. Somehow I thought that Bethesda would be the vehicle God would use to allow me to do that.

"You can imagine, then, the milestone it was for me in 1988. That year, for the first time, Bethesda gave in excess of $1 million to advance God's kingdom. Today, we are giving away $15-20 million annually for that purpose. God's vision is so much bigger than mine.

"That's why I love Ephesians 3:20. This verse is painted on the stairway wall at our headquarters: '*Now glory be to God who by his mighty power at work within us is able to do far more than we would ever dare to ask or even dream of—infinitely beyond our highest prayers, desires, thoughts or hopes,*' (Living Bible). I prayed, I desired and I hoped for that day when we could give away $1 million in a year. But God is going 'infinitely beyond' that."

WHOSE CALL? WHOSE WILL? WHOSE VISION?

David Burdine's story also illustrates the importance of allowing God to define the call, the will and the vision of a leader.

The call of a leader is to do the will of God. The impact of a leader is a direct result of knowing and living for the will of God. That's why it is so important to know the will of God and make a commitment to fulfill His eternal purpose. In such a process, some of the greatest challenges to a leader are his abilities to make distinctions between:

- popularity vs. positive impact,
- busyness vs. effectiveness,
- status vs. functionality,
- authority vs. ministry,
- acceptability vs. obedience, and
- human expectation vs. divine commission.

Therefore, because God calls a leader, His will must shape that leader. It follows, then, that a leader's vision must be defined by God's vision. These seven elements make up the heart of a healthy vision:

1) The source of a true vision is God. Therefore, a leader must focus on his relationship with God to receive and maintain a true vision.
2) Every true vision has its basis in a leader's personal transformation as a result of seeing God.
3) The foundation of a genuine ministry vision is grounded in the ability of a leader to see what God sees.
4) The effectiveness of a vision is the result of knowing what to do and how to do it – as God sees the situation.
5) Godly character – including the willingness to keep growing in the ways and Word of God – is necessary to carry out divine vision.
6) Leaders need to avoid "shortcuts" to action that could short-circuit godly vision. They must wait for God's guidance and persist in prayer.
7) A leader with a healthy vision focuses on working on his character and on his relationships with God and others. The goal: to make Christ and the Kingdom the center of his vision.

A recurring theme emerges in response to the questions, "Whose call? Whose will? Whose vision?" The key is that a leader must surrender to God's call, to God's will and to God's vision each step of the way. Accepting God's call is but the first of many steps in that process of the leadership journey – but without that first step, none of the others would follow.

David Burdine would be among the first to say that such surrender is the right thing to do, at every opportunity. The result is that God's vision often goes "infinitely beyond" a leader's vision. You'll see the pattern not only in David's story, but also in the other leaders' stories in this book.

LESSONS LEARNED

David is very candid about what he has learned about accepting God's calling. As you might expect, his advice has a lot to do with availability.

"If you want to be an emissary to a hurting world ... from the depths of my soul, I say to you, don't try to prove to God how great you are. Just prove how available you are.

"When Sharon and I were first married, we made a commitment to God and to each other that we would 'promise with a big heart and a deep confidence in God.' Whatever role God has for you, don't just talk about your availability. Prove it. Accept His call on your life. The difference is similar to the difference of just having 'Jesus' on your lips – or having His nature in your soul."

Clearly, character building is a high priority for David. So is building bridges between God and a hurting world. That passion drives David to this very day, as he directs Bethesda's missions giving to strategically minister to as many lost and hurting people as possible. David puts this mission clearly: "Shouldn't a leader's focus be to help somebody else?"

David also is a firm believer that God puts visions and dreams before leaders. That's why he encourages people to write down their dreams, to write mission statements and to review them often. He advises, "Even if you don't know exactly where God is taking you, it helps your focus to have dreams and a mission statement. I review mine to this day. God revises them sometimes as He makes His will for specifics clearer to me.

"Activity for its own sake will cause anyone to lose focus. Other people can try, even with good intentions, to put out the fire of the passion God has placed within you. It was like that with my dream of giving away a million dollars a year to missions – very few people empathized with it, much less understood it. So my encouragement is to keep those personal mission statements and dreams within a close circle of family and friends. Always check them out with God and let them help you maintain the focus He wants you to have in response to His calling."

THE PROCESS OF ACCEPTING THE CALL: WHERE DO YOU GO FROM HERE?

David Burdine's story outlines the process of accepting God's calling.

It begins with taking steps of faith. To his credit, even in early leadership David didn't look for a huge roadmap or a guarantee of success. He simply sought to be faithful, one step at a time. He became an accountant. He served in Bethesda. He moved away for a time. In God's season, he accepted the call to return as Bethesda's leader.

You may need to learn, then, to accept God's call as one step in the leadership journey. Perhaps you'll have to give up your desires for a roadmap or guaranteed success from a human perspective.

Stage 2: Accepting the Call

The process continues with being commissioned. In David's case, the commissioning came from God through Bethesda's Board of Directors. He was set apart as a leader to do God's will.

God's call usually comes with a role of service. He often sets people apart for leadership without taking them immediately to the role that will define their career. That's normal. But understand that some role of service will accompany your acceptance of God's calling.

In the middle of a very difficult situation, David received confirmation of his leadership and God's presence. As a result, he was able to function in peace even as he faced great challenges.

Leaders often have to learn to face circumstances only with the promise of God's presence with them. Your confirmation of leadership may come at a point of trial in your life, as it did with David. There are also times when confirmation comes at a point of success.

David also accepted God's will in becoming a leader, and continuing in availability. That led to a series of blessings – divine signs that he followed as he watched God confirm his choice to be available.

Here is the key question for any leader: *Are you available?* That is the question that must be answered even before divine signs confirm your role.

As a result, it became easier for David to make a commitment to the calling. He led Bethesda's Board to a decision to commit a portion of their income to the work of the Kingdom – and God blessed that decision. David remains committed to the calling of God to this day, and is helping others discover God's calling on their lives. It is a special blessing to many who, like David, struggled with the idea of God's calling to something other than "professional ministry."

God's authority comes not by knowing the calling, but by accepting the calling and acting upon it. God then gives a confirmation. Does this eliminate all fear and uncertainty? No, not really. Even after we accept and have seen signs, there's fear or questioning of ourselves as to whether we did the right thing. "Is this real? What is going to happen?" Often, all kinds of questions continue. The most critical thing is to not dwell on our feelings, but to stand on God's promises.

What enables a leader to continue on the journey are not his feelings, but the strength found in the promises of God. That's why Paul, again and again, went back to the calling or experiences he had, and his encounter with Jesus Christ. This is what will help us as we accept the calling. It gives us focus, and with focus the gift will reveal itself. We then can start exercising our gift.

Accepting our gift will bring us to the third stage.

Stage 2: Accepting the Call

QUESTIONS FOR REFLECTION

1. *What do you think the most difficult part of accepting God's call might be for leaders in this stage? For you?*
2. *Why do you suppose God defines leadership in terms of service to others? What might happen to His kingdom if service didn't matter?*

If you are in this stage of the leadership journey, are you willing to accept that God might call you to a profession or career you might not expect as a Christian leader? Explain.

Stage 3
The Leadership Journey

I The Call
Process of >Hearing >Discerning >Promise >From, to and for

II Acceptance
Process of >Step of faith >Entering >Commission >Confirmation >Signs

III Early Leadership
Process of >History >Ministry >People >Team

IV Reality
Process of >Character building >Self discovery >Facing reality >Personal gifts >Call >God >Knowledge

V Maturity
Process of >Building Ministry >Recognizing offices >Correcting History >Making History >Shaping History

VI Value Stage
Process of >Relationship >Building people >Becoming a father >Bearing Fruit >Establishing Pattern

VII Relational Stage
Process of >Relationship >Leaving a legacy

III Early Leadership
Process of
>History
>Ministry
>People
>Team

THE EARLY LEADERSHIP STAGE

"'Come, follow me,' Jesus said, 'and I will make you fishers of men'"
(Matthew 4:19).

Perhaps in His wisdom the Almighty is trying to show us that a leader may chart the way, may point out the road to lasting peace, but that many leaders and many peoples must do the building.
— Eleanor Roosevelt

Throughout history, God has called people and used them as they are to become leaders. He used them with their own personalities and styles intact. However, He continued to build their character so that they would become more like the Lord Jesus Christ.

In the early leadership stage, leaders often struggle with how their leadership styles will fit into God's call on their lives. As their styles are challenged with early tasks and accomplishments, they may begin to doubt whether the call they heard was from God or from their own minds.

These doubts are common to leaders. Yet with God's promptings and promises, many biblical and current leaders were able to accomplish great things in their early leadership years. God allows such success to assure the leaders He chooses that His calling on their lives is authentic. At the same time, these successes demonstrate to leaders that their roles are under the divine authority of God and come about as a result of their submission to God's will.

This early leadership stage is characterized by:
- Understanding people
- Understanding history
- Understanding efficient and effective ministry
- Understanding team

Watch for these themes as you read through chapters five and six.

Chapter 5

Needing to Lead – And Succeed

In the early leadership stage, the Lord brings actual and practical early leadership opportunities. An invitation comes and a person accepts or enters a ministry. It might be starting a ministry or church, becoming a Christian ministry leader or entering the field God has called an individual to.

Early leadership is marked by initial excitement. There's a sense that – finally – what a person has been dreaming about has happened. The anointing of God is upon the leader. An invitation is extended for the leader to take a new job, enter a new country as a missionary, or preach a first message as a pastor. The excitement is a combination of joy, fear and uncertainty about what will happen. It's like the first blush of marriage, a honeymoon time. The vow has been made. The questions arise: Will this marriage continue? Am I going to have a successful marriage? What will happen?

No wonder, then, that in early leadership a person longs for initial success. Seeing the Red Sea divide or killing Goliath is the kind of success and victory individuals look for. That would certainly build their confidence. But there are even greater successes to enjoy in early leadership.

Dutch Sheets is an author and pastor who has warm memories of the lessons he learned during his early leadership years. His story reflects the kind of development God often brings to leaders in early roles of service.

DISCOVERING THE TEAM

"I felt the call to ministry very early in life. Consequently, I took God very seriously at a young age. That didn't prevent me from having a significant time of rebellion in response to a difficult family situation, however. It took about two years to sort that out.

"But by the time I was 19, I felt an incredible sense of destiny. God gave me a firm notion of just how broad the scope of ministry could be. I floundered for four years or so, trying to fulfill God's calling on my life without any idea about how teamwork could benefit the Kingdom, much less my own situation.

"That's when I went to Bible college. I was 23 years old when I made my way to Christ for the Nations for a one-month term. However, I ended up staying for four years – two years as a student and two years as a staff assistant.

"That experience at CFN was the first time I realized that a team was going to be important in my ministry. Bible college exposed me to the broad, multifaceted gifting of the Body of Christ. I was one of 1,200 students and a number of great and dedicated teachers. Everyone was there to discover and use their gifts. Seeing the church as a 'body' – in fact, 'The Body' – really took hold there.

"As a result, I saw that leadership wasn't about building your own spiritual empire. Leadership wasn't even about the size of the group you led. Leadership was about finding the niche God has for you in the whole of His kingdom, then helping others find their niche. That's what matters.

"The fullness of that truth hit home while I was on the CFN staff. I think my title was 'Assistant Director of Student Ministries.' At first, I believed that was a glorified title for a 'go-fer.' But God made it into much more.

"As my title indicated, I helped coordinate student ministries. I had to consider, in prayer and in strategy, just how people could fit together to advance the cause of Christ. I had to think about everyone from quiet teachers' aides to outgoing street evangelists. There were prayer warriors and musicians, worship leaders and sound technicians, children's workers and senior citizen ministers. And God let me see how they all fit together.

"I led a team of 120 students to the Mardi Gras one year. God molded us into a team, and then He let me see that we were a special kind of team – a team coordinated for a purpose.

"One of the New Testament words for 'servant' is the same word used for 'under rower' in a galley ship. Those rowers had to keep a cadence to keep the ship going in the right direction. Their task demanded teamwork. It's a great concept to apply to service in God's kingdom. Think of the synergy, the power of one person's efforts multiplied by teamwork. Then multiply *that* with God's purpose and power.

"I didn't know about the word "synergy" then, but I lived the concept. We all did."

SUCCESS IN EARLY LEADERSHIP

God often gives tangible success in early leadership years. Consider the example of Abraham in Genesis chapters 12–15.

Abraham accepted the call, followed God and agreed to God's purpose. He was willing to sacrifice his comfort zone, leave his relatives and country and go to the country God showed him. In these early days as a leader, God's blessing on Abraham was evident. It began with the promise, "*I will make you into a great nation and I will bless you; I will make your name great, and you will be a blessing,*" (Genesis 12:2).

Abraham's wealth increased. When raiders took his nephew Lot and stole his possessions, Abraham battled them and took it all back – even though it was his first time in such a skirmish. God's promise was reaffirmed in the victory, and in words: "*After this the word of the Lord came to Abram in a vision, 'Do not be afraid, Abram. I am your shield, your very great reward,'*" (Genesis 15:1).

God had singled Abraham out, blessed him materially and given him victory over the enemy. These kinds of blessings are crucial to early leadership. They are positive signs that what God has said is true, and that the leader is indeed called to his or her task.

The material blessings God gives in this stage are not always those that increase one's herds, as was the case with Abraham. For many, the material blessings are the kinds that simply show the leader that God is present and working. These could include a scholarship to begin or continue education, a higher-than-expected salary or even a relationship that profoundly blesses the leader.

Dutch Sheets recalls that God affirmed his call to leadership by giving him unique opportunities to lead at CFN. We're about to see that Dutch's efforts brought CFN students to the frontlines of Great Commission work, where they met with great success. Dutch was blessed by many relationships at CFN, not the least of which was the one that developed with the young lady who was to become his wife.

THE WORK OF THE LEADER

"Back on the CFN campus, my job was to match students with ministry opportunities. The task for the Mardi Gras event wasn't so different – just more complex. I had to coordinate students into teams of two for witnessing, and then assign these teams to groups of ten with a leader. That allowed us to strategically blanket the Mardi Gras with the Gospel in one week.

"We were learning to sow the seed of God's Word together. I was also learning a new niche. Being a leader meant laying down some of the activity I thought was important.

The witnessing teams were coming back daily with wonderful reports of leading people to Christ. But during our entire time at the Mardi Gras, I didn't lead one person to Jesus. I didn't witness all week.

"My task on the team was different. I was the coordinator. I was one of the prayer warriors. That week it was more important for me to serve in the background than in public. I let the team members see me pray for them. I rejoiced with them, talked them through some challenges and encouraged them to encourage each other. It was the first time I led by doing something different than my teammates, and it revolutionized my notion of leadership."

EFFICIENCY AND EFFECTIVENESS

There is another lesson to learn from King David in early leadership. His early success was marked by two characteristics: efficiency and effectiveness. Efficiency and effectiveness mark any good organization – and should become character traits in developing leaders.

In early leadership, when a person depends on God and moves under God's guidance and the anointing of the Holy Spirit, that individual has both of these characteristics. In David's case, he picked five stones to use against Goliath and only used one. In language an accountant would appreciate, David used 20 percent of his stones and had 80 percent left over. This was efficiency. Concerning effectiveness, David threw only once and killed the giant. That was effectiveness. The anointing of the Holy Spirit brings both of these characteristics into a leader's life. In early leadership, God gives as His blessing and as a sign success in both effectiveness and efficiency if a leader operates under the anointing and with the right motive and attitude.

You'll notice much the same sense of efficiency and effectiveness in Dutch's account of his coordinating the Mardi Gras ministry during his time at CFN. It took efficiency to coordinate the ministry teams, the group leaders and their activities. The effectiveness of the effort was proven in the changed lives that resulted from CFN's ministry that week.

Discovering and implementing efficient and effective leadership often results in the successes that are benchmarks of the early leadership stage.

Chapter 6

Meeting Early Leadership Challenges

Dutch Sheets came to CFN with the knowledge that he wasn't complete in himself. In his own words, he sensed he was "floundering." He was ready to find a team and to develop leadership skills as a servant to others.

Many who are in the early leadership stage have yet to accept these truths. Like Dutch, God has given us a degree of success to build our confidence and fulfill the calling. But until we seek to embrace the lessons God will teach us in early leadership, we will face a number of challenges. If we aren't careful, some of the issues can bring discouragement and lead to serious problems.

In early leadership, the biggest challenge to a leader is his or her inner desire for success. Every leader who accepts a call of God has a built-in desire for success. The temptation here is to lead in our own way, prove that *we* can do it and completely ignore God's direction. This is very dangerous. We see this in the life of King Saul and his want to succeed in war against the Philistines. He told Samuel, the priest and prophet of God, to come and make the sacrifice for the battle. When Samuel didn't show up according to Saul's timetable, Saul made the sacrifice himself – an act for which he was completely unqualified. This brought disaster on his leadership and his downfall began that day. The desire for success is dangerous if it is not controlled and channeled appropriately.

A second challenge in early leadership is the temptation to focus on impressing others. In early leadership this is often a tactic to gain acceptability or approval. Young leaders attempt to impress others by the way they talk, act or plan. The desire to gain acceptability by impressing others sometimes leads them to exaggerate. At the very least, when we try to impress we listen to what people say or don't say or what they like or don't like – and often miss what God would have us do.

In early leadership a leader can long for popularity. In this stage young leaders are usually tempted to compare themselves to other leaders who are successful, loved or popular. Young leaders will try to copy those leaders they admire and are successful. The problem is this: *Popularity and fulfilling the purpose of God usually don't fit together well.* We would do well to remember that as Jesus continued in the Father's will, He grew less – not more – popular. A leader should pray for God's favor, not popularity.

Young leaders are very energetic. This can lead to a fourth challenge: lack of balance. Because of all their energy, young leaders often want to get everything accomplished overnight. This energy must be directed toward the purpose of God and how God wants it used. Without proper direction, this kind of energy can cause young leaders to "run ahead" with their ministry. The result? They usually end up losing others on their team because not everyone is so energetic. A pattern of running off by oneself, combined with an unwillingness to wait for others, becomes a dangerous problem. It can convince a leader that he or she is, indeed, alone in doing God's work, which results in an unbalanced life and ministry.

The fifth challenge for young leaders is vision and expectation. Young leaders are full of God-given vision for their tasks. Because they're able to see things, they tend to say, "I've seen it and I want it today." But vision is not given to enable one to get something done within 24 hours. Vision is for providing direction. It's knowing what we're here for, where we are to go, what's possible and knowing the potential. A leader has to be careful how he or she handles vision.

Pride is another challenge for a young leader. Pride stemming from one's education or experience can cause that individual to avoid wise counsel. Pride is also used to hide one's lack of self-confidence. Though the person wants to be accepted, wants to impress and be popular, he or she still lacks self-confidence – a situation that often leads to pride.

The challenge of indispensability is the seventh challenge for a young leader. Due to God's blessing and activity in the early leadership stage, a young leader can begin to see himself as being indispensable: "Since I've become a leader, look at everything that's been happening! God couldn't operate the Kingdom without me!" This attitude – simply another form of pride – usually leads to failure. Unless a person has this under control, he sees himself as essential to the organization's vision, energy and success.

Independence is another challenge to the young leader. Because of success in early leadership, young leaders sometimes desire to become independent. They feel that they don't need anyone and can do it themselves. With this independent feeling, especially when coupled with popularity, the leader is tempted to do everything himself. He gets involved in everything and has to have total control. He has to be everywhere and attend every meeting. It's hard for him to give responsibilities to others. Delegating authority is especially difficult because the leader wants independence and feels he needs to know everything. This attitude is risky because it can lead to burnout.

As strange as this may sound, a high level of commitment is the ninth challenge facing young leaders. A leader is naturally committed to the calling, the ministry and usually to the people he serves. If the commitment level is too high, a leader stretches himself beyond his capabilities. Because the energy is there, the young leader thinks he can reach and take care of everyone. Yet quite often a leader is very naïve about reality at this stage. He works with head knowledge and lacks wisdom. He tries to touch every aspect of the ministry and, as a result, overextends himself. This is another situation that easily leads to burnout.

The tenth challenge in early leadership is an idealistic view of the ministry and of oneself. A person's knowledge or vision hasn't yet been tested, so everything is idealistic. That idealistic view looks at the perfect picture, without understanding the reality of potential pain. If a person isn't careful, he'll soon discover pain – bringing into his life discouragement and certain feelings of hopelessness. This becomes a time when a person questions if he's been called, if he's in God's will and why he's in the situation.

In the early leadership stage the person is also working with untested knowledge, yet another challenge for the young leader. He has knowledge, but it's "book knowledge," not knowledge that is based on experience. A young leader thinks has the answer for everything – without understanding that it takes time for book knowledge to be tested and proven workable. This is frequently a problem with young leaders when they leave seminary and go into ministry. They have an idealistic approach as to what the church should be like and how it is to function. They soon see a discrepancy between what they've learned in seminary versus the reality of the community they find themselves in, and this leads to frustration.

A young leader usually works with untested gifts, the twelfth challenge in this stage. A person feels he has a gift, but because it is untested, the individual's confidence level isn't very high. Because a leader at this stage is concerned with success, this leads to the next challenge: fear.

Fear is a profound challenge to a young leader. Because of untested knowledge and spiritual gifts, a person fears failure, or fears the unknown. He questions whether he'll be a success or a failure. He continually wonders: *What will happen?* This results in deep insecurity. Even when a leader uses his gifts, he's not sure the gifts will accomplish what they're intended for. Fear is a challenge that must be dealt with every day. Fear is only conquered by remembering the calling and trusting God's commission to him. It comes back to what the Lord said to Jeremiah when he called him: *"Do not say 'I am only a child.' You must go to everyone I send you to and say whatever I command you. Do not be afraid...for I am with you...Then the Lord reached out his hand and touched my mouth and said to me, 'Now, I have put my words in your mouth,'"* (Jeremiah 1:7-9). The words that need to be repeated to early leaders is this: *"Fear not."*

Criticism of others is another challenge for young leaders. Particularly in early leadership it's easy to be critical of people. It's tempting to harshly criticize how something was done in the past without fully understanding the challenge of why it had been done in the way it was. Unless he guards himself against developing a critical spirit, it's easy to criticize past methods. This almost always creates tension between the leader and his followers. The most important approach for the leader at this stage is not to necessarily accept everything that's been done, but to look at it carefully and with appreciation, and then suggest possible changes.

Lack of patience is the fifteenth challenge in early leadership. The young leader sees what needs to be done. His vision is clear, his energy is at its peak – and that is when it becomes easy to lose patience. It's a challenge to balance what a young leader envisions with how to win over people who are set in their ways and convert them to his way of thinking. This is the challenge the young leader faces – and it takes patience.

The sixteenth challenge is how to handle success. It may not sound like a challenge, but success actually *is* a challenge. In early leadership there's energy, vision, excitement and signs of success from God. The challenge is how to handle success. Success in early leadership can cause young leaders to see themselves as indispensable. They are tempted to "rest on their laurels" when their leadership journey has barely begun! Due to lack of experience, most young leaders don't know how to deal with success, and often isolate themselves from others instead of discovering the value of teamwork and others' gifts. As a result, they fail to move on to the next stage of leadership.

If you review this list of challenges, you'll notice that most of them have to do with the need of the young leader to revise his or her expectations of what leadership means. Dutch Sheets experienced great success in early leadership because he embraced the process of letting God show him the true nature of leadership. Let's continue with his story.

THE "AHA!" OF EARLY LEADERSHIP

"It surprised me to find out how much leadership has to happen in the background. No one modeled that better for me than Gordon Lindsey, who headed up CFN. He lived out the truth that leadership was often a background activity. He constantly brought in others to lead student chapels.

He encouraged popular authors and speakers to lead classes. He even gave CFN's magazine to others when he felt the time was right.

"Gordon Lindsey showed me that a leader had to see to it that others were being equipped. He let me see that a leader's ongoing objective was to get others into the forefront. That really impressed me.

"So if a leader is working to develop a team, you try to develop the best in team dynamics. You encourage variety. In the church that means you celebrate and utilize men and women, a variety of cultures and a variety of servants: missionaries, pastors, evangelists, teachers. It's crucial to have both variety and balance on the team.

"And I also learned how critical it is for you to under gird all of your team with prayer."

FACING CHALLENGES WITH AUTHORITY

Moses' early leadership challenges began after the Israelites came out of Egypt and faced the Red Sea. The people were afraid when they saw Pharaoh and his military chasing them. When they looked ahead, there was the Red Sea. They started complaining. Moses' first challenge came, so God reminded Moses that He had given him authority. God told him to get up and act, and He would again give Moses victory. He would confirm that Moses was the chosen leader to take the people into the Promised Land. Moses stretched his hand and the Red Sea divided. In Exodus 14:15 is a powerful phrase, *"Then the Lord said to Moses, 'Why are you crying out to me? Tell the Israelites to move on."* Since he was in leadership, there was no time to cry. It was time to act and take the people to their destination. God was telling Moses to use his authority.

Early leadership is when a leader starts using his God-given, divine authority. The test comes in trusting God and using the divine authority properly.

The proper use of authority depends much on understanding *divine* authority. The most important thing for a young leader is not how much he can accomplish using authority or power, but his understanding of divine authority and power. In early leadership, a leader who understands authority will submit to authority. Authority comes through submitting to authority. Thus, a person will have more authority by submitting to divine authority. Submission provides protection and covering.

When the apostle Paul encountered Jesus Christ, he understood authority. On the road to Damascus God gave him a chance, in that first encounter, to understand authority. This is why Paul asked, "Who are you?" He basically was trying to establish authority, or the line of authority. He needed to understand who God was and accept that authority. Once that authority was established, Paul immediately responded, "What would you have me do?" He submitted to that authority – he no longer cared about his own Damascus agenda.

When Paul asked what the Lord wanted him to do, the Lord answered and said, "Go to the city and you will be told what to do." God was saying to Paul that divine authority is one thing, but he also needed to understand human authority. *You will be told.* And again, Paul submitted himself to authority. When he arrived at the city, a brother came to him. Though Paul was called to be an apostle, still the brother came and laid hands on him and said, "Paul, the Lord that you saw on the road to Damascus, the same Lord has sent me to you." He was affirming what the Lord Jesus said.

In the same way, a young leader needs to be under both the Lord's authority and human authority. This is the most important factor. That's where Paul started and this pattern of submission runs throughout his ministry.

We see the same thing in Jesus' life. When the time came to go out and minister, Jesus placed himself under the authority of John the Baptist. He came to the Jordan River and was baptized by John. Though Jesus was greater than John, He still submitted to John's authority.

A person or leader only understands authority when he's willing to die to self before he steps into what God has called him to do. The challenge in early leadership is that instead of dying, the person tries to survive, thrive, demonstrate and prove. Contrary to this, power and authority *can* be exercised through death. The more we die to self, the more God reveals himself through us. Paul refers to this in Galatians 2:20: "*I have been crucified with Christ.*" Paul was a powerful servant of the Living God, and an apostle of the Lord Jesus, yet he proclaimed, "I don't live, but Christ lives in me."

This is the source of authority: dying to self and the willingness to put oneself under the covering of others. This leads to instruction, direction, correction, challenges and encouragement – all of which are necessary in order to correctly use authority.

What shapes a leader's ministry is how a leader uses his authority during early leadership. Some overuse it. Others don't use it enough. But more than a few misuse it. Sometimes a leader denies the authority. Here is where young leaders need mentors. Guidance, encouragement and balance are greatly needed at this point.

In addition to apostolic fathering, prophetic guidance is also greatly needed during this early leadership stage. In regard to this point, there is a very powerful verse in 2

Chronicles 26:5: *"He sought God during the days of Zechariah, who instructed him in the fear of God. As long as he sought the Lord, God gave him success."* The "he" in this verse is young King Uzziah. The prophet Zechariah taught the young leader the fear of the Lord and as a result, the young king purposed in his heart to seek the Lord and become successful. Later he stopped listening to the voice of the prophets and rejected the advice of the priests. It was at that point that he turned the great success of his beginning into a failure at the end. Even for a king, willingness to submit to authority is critically important.

In early leadership, success is critical for the leader. However, how a leader uses his authority will determine how successful the leader will be the remainder of his life.

David was called to be king, was anointed and accepted the anointing. In the early confirmation of his acceptance he was able to kill a lion and bear. This basically confirmed that the presence, power and protection of God were with him. God then brought him to the position He prepared for him.

During early leadership David didn't come to lead the Israelites. Instead he came to visit his brothers. While visiting his brothers, he saw what was happening. His first battle was with his own brother, whose heart God rejected. David knew who he was. He knew his calling and that the hand of God was upon him. He recalled how God had protected him while fighting the animals, so now he realized that if God could protect him from vicious animals, He could protect him from a person – the giant who insulted the people of God and put down God's name. David was willing to go fight the giant.

The first obvious characteristic of David's early leadership was his willingness to trust the Lord. David wasn't seeking a position, but he was ready to operate under the anointing. In this context, there are two factors. First there is the *position*, and second there is the *authority* of the office. David didn't have an actual position as king, but he did have the authority of a king because the anointing of God was upon him. He said he wasn't going to confront the giant simply because of his position. He would face the giant because of the office God had called him to, and the anointing of God that was upon him.

In early leadership this issue is usually missed. Most leaders wait for the position before they act for God – but the anointing and authority is with the individual once he accepts the calling. Sometimes if young leaders don't understand this concept, they may not use their authority. They may even fight for a position and run the risk of losing God's anointing. They feel that since God called them and they've accepted the anointing, then the position should be vacated for them to fill. This is not necessarily true. There is a process and time factor. David didn't fight for the position, or because of it. Rather he fought the giant with the authority God had given him. Thus David brought down the giant and killed him by using the authority God had given him as a result of the anointing upon his life.

Second, David didn't use the armor or sword of Saul. He used what he had – stones, a sling and his experience. One of the temptations in early leadership is trying to copy leaders who have gone before. This is dangerous and it is how the enemy tried to divert the purpose of God in David's life. When Saul offered David his own armor, David put it on but he couldn't carry it. It was a protective shield for Saul, but for David it was a burden.

A leader must be discerning about what he receives. If a leader receives something that is not from the Lord, it's not a protective shield or armor, it is a burden that could destroy the anointing or his ability to act for God. David told Saul he couldn't kill the giant with the heavy metal armor on him. Thus David took the armor off. The success of David came not when he threw the stone, but when he took off Saul's armor. It did not belong on him.

It is tempting to copy a successful leader. Sometimes a person has the temptation to take on another's style of management, speaking or personality. God does not want this. God doesn't call a leader to be the duplicate of another. God calls people and uses them as they are, with their own personalities and styles. We are called to be like Jesus in terms of character, and to be true to the new creation we are in Jesus in terms of everything else.

The call of a leader is to humble himself under the hand of the Lord, so God can exalt or lift him up for His purpose or for what God wants to do in his life.

Dutch Sheets had a wonderful experience in early leadership. He submitted to what the CFN staff and leaders could teach him, exercised authority in a genuine "classroom of the Holy Spirit," and learned the power of submitting every detail of life and leadership to God in prayer. In that way, Dutch brought the authority of God to bear on every situation possible.

It doesn't get much better than that.

SERVICE AND THE CALL TO LEADERSHIP

Dutch Sheets' story makes this clear: *The call to Christian leadership implies responsibility for others.* This aspect makes Christian leadership distinct among other types of leadership.

Why? Because accepting the responsibility for others begins with true service. This kind of attitude permeates not only Dutch's example, but each of the modern and biblical leaders used as examples for positive Christian leadership in this book. It boils down to this: *A person who doesn't know how to serve isn't qualified to lead.*

Leadership is a lifestyle as much as skills, traits or gifts. The main aspect of leadership is character. That's why the Lord spends so much time in the leadership journey in the character-building process. A leadership call that is based on total obedience to the revealed will of God means the leader will serve God and others wholeheartedly through his or her spiritual gifting and the anointing of the Holy Spirit. These are powerful instruments in the hand of God.

The biblical model of leadership engages *function* more than *stature*. Dutch Sheets was just as effective in the economy of God's kingdom in his days as a coordinator of student activities as he would be in later life because he was fulfilling the purpose of God at that time. Fulfilling the purpose of God is the core of a leader's call.

Leadership authority is attained through serving rather than ruling. One's position is not as important as one's specific calling to carry out the will of God. In any leadership calling it is crucial to recognize God's authority in your own life and in others. These principles set the foundation for the lessons of early leadership Dutch Sheets learned in his journey.

LESSONS LEARNED

Dutch Sheets is clear about the value of the lessons he learned during these early leadership years.

"The time at CFN and my role as a ministry coordinator absolutely established the value and need of prayer in my life as a leader. It also taught me how important it is to perceive your role as a leader in terms of service. The idea isn't to put yourself in the public eye, but to promote others in service to the Kingdom.

"I also learned the importance of people and their roles in teamwork. That led to much greater efficiency in my role as a leader and a far more effective ministry than I could ever achieve on my own.

"It's not the visibility or seeming importance of a task that defines effective ministry. What matters is that each one does his or her part well – and a leader has the responsibility to help each one do just that.

"These lessons mean more to me than any theology I learned, as wonderful as that teaching was. I learned to pray, to become a worshiper – and that to lead is to serve."

WHERE CAN YOU GO FROM HERE?

Early leadership is marked by four points of understanding.

Understanding people is crucial. Here, a leader must learn how to read the gifts and personalities of others. It is a vital element of building a team, and just as important, tends to take the leader's focus off himself and on to others.

You probably noticed that Dutch Sheets actually delighted in his growing understanding of people and their potential in this stage. If you find yourself in this stage and your style of leadership is still largely self-focused, it's likely you need to pay greater attention to this discipline.

Understanding history is also an important element in this stage. The question here is whether the leader embraces the fact that God uses people as they are. He works to build the character of Christ in each one, but calls people to specific tasks because he has given them specific gifts. Moses wasn't Abraham. David wasn't Joseph. Deborah wasn't Priscilla.

John the Baptist wasn't the apostle Paul. Yet each one had a specific task to bring his or her generation closer to God.

Dutch Sheets took particular note of the tradition at CFN during this stage. He thrived on the fact that a variety of ministry took place because God had placed a variety of people at CFN – and that very fact liberated Dutch to develop his own style of leadership during his time at CFN. Probably one of the most important issues for a young leader to grasp is that God has placed specific gifts and attributes in them that suit them for the task He has called the leader to accomplish. No young leader needs to be a copy of another leader. If you are pursuing leadership by trying to adopt the style of someone else, you will probably benefit from a time of earnest prayer with God to discover more about who He is making you to be.

Understanding efficient and effective ministry often marks this stage. Many times early successes for biblical leaders depended upon efficiency and effectiveness, as we demonstrated in the example of David's battle with Goliath. Yet one of the key lessons to learn here is that efficient and effective ministry rarely, if ever, happens if a leader relies solely on his or her personal resources. David had to lean on God's power for his encounter with the giant. Jesus coordinated His disciples into ministry teams to feed the multitudes. It wasn't that these leaders couldn't have tried to do everything themselves – it's just that they understood that God worked through efficiency and effectiveness.

To bring efficiency and effectiveness to any situation, a leader has to engage in background work. The leader must think in terms of efficiency and effectiveness to make the best use of God's resources – human and otherwise. That may not be the kind of ministry he or she anticipated, but it is, nonetheless, a crucial part of leadership development. If you have yet to think of God's work through you in these terms, perhaps it's time you did.

Finally, the early leadership stage is characterized by *understanding teamwork*. The way Jesus administered ministry teams among His disciples is evidence that God himself places a high value on teamwork. For Jesus, teamwork meant that His disciples would take the frontlines of ministry – exactly the preparation they needed to lead the Church.

Dutch Sheets is a powerful preacher. (I know – he's my pastor!) He could have kept himself at the forefront of many ministry situations at CFN. People would have been added to the Kingdom. But that wasn't his role at the time. As a leader, he knew he would need to develop effective teams for ministry. The variety of gifts and people that could be brought into a situation would far surpass anything he might try to do alone. In the same way, if you haven't worked on a team – or haven't developed a team – you're missing one of the most important steps in early leadership.

These points of understanding are vital to any leader as the force of the next stage enters their journey. They dare not be ignored.

QUESTIONS FOR REFLECTION

1. *What surprises you the most about the discoveries a leader makes in this stage of the leadership journey: understanding people, history, effective ministry, or teams? Why?*
2. *Do you think of "success" only in terms of position, or in terms of function? Explain.*

If you are in this stage of the leadership journey, what successes do you see God giving you to confirm His call on your life? Are they enough to convince you?

Stage 4
The Leadership Journey

I The Call
Process of >Hearing >Discerning >Promise >From, to and for

II Acceptance
Process of >Step of faith >Entering >Commission >Confirmation >Signs

III Early Leadership
Process of >History >Ministry >People >Team

IV Reality
Process of >Character building >Self discovery >Facing reality >Personal gifts >Call >God >Knowledge

V Maturity
Process of >Building Ministry >Recognizing offices >Correcting History >Making History >Shaping History

VI Value Stage
Process of >Relationship >Building people >Becoming a father >Bearing Fruit >Establishing Pattern

VII Relational Stage
Process of >Relationship >Leaving a legacy

IV Reality
Process of
>Character building
>Self discovery
>Facing reality
>Personal gifts
>Call
>God
>Knowledge

THE REALITY STAGE

*"Come to me, all you who are weary and burdened,
and I will give you rest"*
(Matthew 11:28).

*"I have lived long enough to be battered by the realities of life
and not too long to be downed by them."*
– John Mason Brown

Sometimes early successes can lead a young leader to believe he or she is in control; that he or she has become the very reason for the successful experiences.

In the belief that they have everything figured out, young leaders might even forget to ask the Lord for His will in everyday matters. That could be why the reality check brought about in the next stage of the leadership journey is so important.

The truth of a leader's strengths and weaknesses is shown in the reality stage. The truth will reveal that instead of "having arrived" as a leader, the leader's journey has, in fact, only just begun.

God uses circumstances, people and situations to build a leader's character. The reality of these elements will introduce the leader to a time of transition: from *knowing* to *practicing* that which has been learned; from *doing* leadership activities to *being* a leader; and from *serving one's own purposes* to *building the kingdom of God.*

This transition makes the reality stage the time a leader can begin to make history. It matures the leader by refocusing that individual on God rather than on personal success.

These characteristics mark the process of the reality stage:
- Self-discovery: personal gifts, strengths, and weaknesses
- Discovering the reality of a personal call
- Discovery of God
- Discovery of applied knowledge
- Character building

Watch for these themes as you review chapters seven and eight.

Chapter 7

Taking a Long, Hard Look at Yourself

It is easy for young leaders to look at their successes and begin to think, "I've arrived. I'm a fully developed leader now!"

Though it's easy, it's also a deception.

Young leaders often believe their early successes are a mark of maturity and control. There's a temptation to forget God's hand in your role as a leader. You look instead to your own understanding. You might even believe that you have everything figured out.

That's why there's a reality stage in every leader's journey. It's the time when the leader confronts the reality of his or her personal limitations.

Mulatu Belachew, a longtime leader in Kingdom concerns in Africa, has worked in the worlds of local church leadership as a lay pastor, in banking and in relief and development alike. Presently he serves as the Africa Area Director for Compassion International in Nairobi, Kenya. In the next two chapters Mulatu recalls the time when reality hit home in his own leadership journey.

THE HARD, LONG LOOK

"I started my career at a bank in Asmara, then a city in northern Ethiopia (now a part of Eritrea). It was 1969. I had been a Christian for some time.

"At the bank, I had become accustomed to thinking about leadership in terms of *position*. But I was to discover that in Christian leadership, an emphasis on *process* had to be made.

"Simply put, that meant that I had to lose any sense of 'having arrived.' My successes could not hinge on a leadership position. I had to rediscover leadership as a perpetual learner. I had to see myself and others in process – the process of gaining knowledge through experience . . . the process of following our callings in an attempt to follow the Lord.

"The biggest shift for me was moving away from the idea that leadership meant making decisions on my own. I had to learn how to lean on God for help, and how He could use others to help me in decision-making.

"My 'wake-up call' was an invitation to be a church elder while I was still working at the bank. I asked, 'What does it involve?' A missionary at the church answered, 'It's about following the Master. What we are asking you to do is to walk with the Lord and to learn from Him.'

"The missionary saw the potential in me and he discipled me into a deeper walk with the Lord. He really invested in me at a time when I needed investment. You see, to that point I had never seen myself as a leader. But he began to point out that I was often in the context of leading. Others expected me to offer counsel or to take the lead in a project. One thing we both agreed on was that I could learn much more.

"I had to deal with the truth that others were more mature in their faith than I was. I had to trust others' judgment more than before – certainly more than I felt I could at the bank. The more I looked at my liabilities and the degree to which I needed to grow, the less secure I felt. But my missionary friend was one of those people who could sell a refrigerator to an Eskimo — and more important, he was willing to be a model for me.

"He was a tremendous motivator. He was very vulnerable. He allowed me to see everything about his style of leadership. He showed me time and again that leadership is a process. He was one of the few people God brought into my life for the purpose of discipling me. He helped me put the practical aspect of leadership from my context at the bank into the context of the Kingdom.

"I also remember one time I became very upset with a church issue and wanted to inject some more business sense into what was going on. I insisted the issue be resolved immediately, and couldn't see why others were opposed to that. My missionary friend took me outside and said, 'Welcome to the club! You need to learn how to deal with this.' I had been looking back to my comfort zone in business for the answer when the situation called for looking forward to the Lord's solution to the issue. It would be new territory for all of us involved — me included.

"The missionary used that instance to show me that in business, I was very procedure- or system-oriented. I was accustomed to issuing a prescription for everything. As a manager in the secular business world, that's what they paid me to do. Don't misunderstand me; I still believe that many churches could benefit from management decision processes. I believe firmly that most of the churches I have encountered would gain much from taking a more systematic approach to problems.

"Yet the church — indeed, the kingdom of God — is different than the business arena. Leaders need to respect the fact that we deal with people who are voluntarily gathered in response to God's call. It's a totally different dynamic. Leaders in a Kingdom context must realize they deal with others as fellow travelers, not employees. That makes

Kingdom leadership far more difficult. We must be responsive not to a system, but to what God is doing in each life.

"If that doesn't bring you into a reality check regarding your own strengths and weaknesses – and your own need to depend upon God rather than your own resources – very little else will."

WHEN THE HONEYMOON IS OVER

Character building time! As Mulatu Belachew's story unfolds, it's clear to see the challenges of the reality stage in the leadership journey.

Each stage of the journey has its own focus. For example, the calling stage focus is hearing the promises of God. God speaks in various ways. Once we hear His voice, we accept the calling. The hearing of the promises and calling of God are extremely important at the calling stage.

A leader then moves to the acceptance stage. During this stage, the most important element is the presence of God, confirmed by His giving the gift(s) necessary for a leader to accept the calling.

During the early leadership stage, a leader's focus often turns to knowledge – the "how-tos" of leadership, affirmed by God granting early successes. The leader may sense there is little left to learn due to his or her track record to date.

That's why I believe the reality stage is so critical in God's design. In the reality stage the focus is power. It's easy for a leader to reach the reality stage and think, "I have been successful in early leadership, so now I am in control." God wants a person to know much more than power. In the reality stage God wants the person to not only know the work, He wants to bring the individual into a deeper knowledge of *Him*. God wants to move a person from early leadership success – with its untested knowledge and gifts – to

Stage 4: The Reality Stage

the reality stage. In this way He can start building the leader's character.

At its core, the reality stage is a character building stage. It is rare for any leader to enjoy this stage. That should come as no surprise. If we are honest with ourselves, the reality stage is a major challenge.

In early leadership, the person was very successful, the honeymoon was on, and everything was at its peak. Suddenly people start challenging and asking the leader, "What are you doing? Who do you think you are?" That was the irony Mulatu faced as an elder of the church. He was asked to exercise leadership as part of a team in that context, yet he was challenged when he desired to apply more business theory to a local church issue. The honeymoon period was over and the reality challenges were settling in. But Mulatu was certainly not the first leader to face such challenges.

Let's consider the example of Moses. God gave him early success. Moses was able to perform miracles in Egypt. More than once, God proved His presence was with Moses during his leadership. When Israel came to the Red Sea, God told Moses to use the authority given him. As a leader, Moses took the staff in his hand and divided the Red Sea, and Israel crossed the seabed to escape the Egyptian army. That was his early success. Forty years were still facing them, but Moses was very pleased in this early success. Not only Moses, but also his sister Miriam and the rest of the Israelites picked up instruments and started singing and praising the Lord. There was a great celebration over the victory and success stemming from the Red Sea experience (Exodus 15).

As can be typical of success in early leadership, Moses went through a time where he didn't seek the Lord. Along the journey, the people started asking about water — and much more. They said they had come from Egypt, from the land of slavery, and the Lord had divided the Red Sea to help them escape. God had punished their enemies, but that was then. They were in the wilderness now. What will life be like in the wilderness? What do they eat? What do they drink?

The reality stage started settling in. The performing of miracles was over. What was there to drink now? Where is the water? Because of Moses' early success and experiences in the wilderness, he didn't ask the Lord for advice. This is where the first hard lesson of reality set in for Moses. Due to past success in early leadership, a leader usually lacks the wisdom to go to the Lord and ask, "What do you have for me? How should I do this? How do I respond to people's questions?"

After Moses cried to the Lord out of fear of Pharaoh's military and the Red Sea, the Lord showed him what to do. When the people then asked him what to drink and where do they go from there, he answered on his own: "There is no water."

Moses didn't ask the Lord about the issue, nor did he pray. He didn't seek the face of the Lord. Instead, he started depending on his personal experiences. Because he lived in the wilderness for so long, Moses knew exactly where to find water. He directed the people of Israel to walk until they reached the place called "Marah." There, they would find water.

I must emphasize again that Moses didn't ask the Lord if Israel should walk there or not. Based on his own personal experiences, knowledge and confidence, he started leading the people to Marah. He had stopped asking the Lord about much of anything. That was one of Moses' failures. As a consequence, it was as though the Lord said to

Moses, "Character building time! Now you are going to enter the reality stage. You will face some challenges."

Israel walked for three days without water. It was very difficult walking in the wilderness. The group was composed of all ages. They had no water, because Moses didn't take time to ask the Lord. When they came to Marah, where Moses thought they'd find water, it wasn't drinkable: *"For three days they traveled in the desert without finding water. When they came to Marah, they could not drink its water because it was bitter,"* (Exodus 15:22,23).

How would you feel after a three-day journey through the wilderness without water – and then once your leader had promised you a drink, you found out it was bitter? It's no wonder the people grumbled against Moses and said, *"Now* what are we to drink?" We must remember that this promise of water was Moses' promise, not God's promise. The people still did not turn to God, but they *did* turn against Moses.

This was the reality check. Until now, particularly after performing the final miracles, meaning the Passover and Red Sea, everything seemed great. There was singing, praise, and excitement. But now the honeymoon was over. Reality had hit. They turned on Moses and attempted to stone him. At the end of his own resources – exactly the place God wanted him – Moses finally turned to the Lord and asked what to do. He cried out to the Lord.

The Lord showed Moses a piece of wood, a stick. God told him to throw the stick into the water. When Moses followed God's direction, the water became sweet. This is symbolic of what God does. The solution came from God. After reality set in, God showed Moses he had to learn to ask and depend on Him. Moses was not to look back at personal experiences or successes in the past. If Moses was to lead God's people, he had to learn to depend on God.

There is also a symbolic lesson here. When Moses put the stick in the water, the water became sweet. This prophetically points to the cross of Christ. The bitterness of life and experiences in the wilderness can be transformed because of the Cross. Unless Christ is in it, human experience is very bitter. Human promises are very bitter. A leader cannot give a sweet and satisfying promise to the people he leads. Satisfaction comes through the cross of Christ.

This is why a leader needs to keep a close relationship with the Lord. This was Moses' experience. He was challenged and the Lord provided a means. After this was over, they had water to drink and were happy. God gave them the word and His promises came. They started moving on, but the challenges didn't stop there. From that time on until the death of Moses, they continued to challenge him for forty years. Through this, God was building Moses' character. The reality stage is therefore a character-building stage, a time to get in touch with our gifts, knowledge, responsibilities, personal character and the character of others. It is character-building reality.

It is the reality Mulatu Belachew experienced in his own leadership journey as he adjusted his expectations of what it means to be a Christian leader. In the next chapter we join Mulatu as he continues with his story.

Chapter 8

Letting God Mold, Build and Strengthen Your Character

"*Understanding what God is doing*: here is the key challenge in Christian leadership. How is God working out the principles of the Kingdom in the lives of those around you? In your own life? It is a frightening position for leaders, because God is at work and invites me to join Him as I make decisions.

"The reality of maturing leadership will make you shift from a dependency on yourself, or your systems, to a greater dependence on God. You become humbled by – and through – the process, and that is a part of your maturity. You surrender your independence. I did. I had no choice.

"The greatest problem in leadership is a sense of pride, a sense that 'I know it all.' That leads to a leader asking, 'Why do I have to wait on God or pray?'

"The paradox of leadership is the fact that you will become more decisive as you grow. At the same time, you go through more waiting on God.

"I began learning these lessons in 1969, but I still pray for God to give me the ability to self-evaluate. I pray to face every situation so it gives glory to God. That is why I began to learn not to fear failure. George, the elder who was my mentor, made it clear that failure could produce a good lesson, because failure usually causes us to turn to God.

"Every biblical leader had to face failure. Yet a close relationship with God can change the face of failure. In fact, that relationship should also remind the leader that facing reality means that you need to realize your giftedness as well. A leader's self-evaluation should not focus exclusively on weaknesses. There is also a profound need to determine and exercise your strengths to God's glory. This part of leadership begins in a prayer closet, on your knees. But exercising your giftedness is liberating, as few other things can be.

"I remember one performance evaluation I went through while I was facing the realities of leadership. God had taken me through a process where He clearly convinced me that deliberation and analysis were high on the list of gifts He intended me to use.

"The evaluation was very positive. Yet most of us feel that even in a very positive evaluation, we have room to grow. That one was no exception. My supervisor mentioned, almost in passing at the end of our session, 'Some people here have commented that you're not as aggressive a decision maker as you could be.'

"I received that as a compliment. God had taken me to the point where I understood the gifts He'd given me. I was able to reply, 'That will not change. I make decisions in a certain way. I think in a deliberate fashion when it is needed. I understand that I'm not always needed to think in that way, and I'm not threatened by that.'

"There was no need for me to be defensive. There was no need to attack anyone's observation about me. I knew God was using that aspect of who I was according to His will, and that others would also be used in their capacities. But that kind of self-understanding only came from spending a lot of time with God, asking Him to build my character and use the gifts He'd placed in me."

DISCIPLINE AND DISCOVERY

Mulatu Belachew discovered much about his own gifting and God's purpose for him during the reality stage of his leadership journey. So did David.

When David killed Goliath, Israel rejoiced and celebrated. David became a public hero. David was delighted, but Saul, Israel's king at the time of the victory, became angry. David's success caused jealousy to rise up in Saul. The reality stage started setting in for David.

David became a fugitive from Saul, who continually tried to kill him. The honeymoon period was now over for David. The people of Israel were set free from the tyranny of the Philistines, but in this reality stage, David's leadership and life alike were at great risk. God had made His call known to David. He had anointed him, given him power and talent, and David then conquered the giant. But there's something else God needed to do in David's life: He needed to build David's character. And God began working in David's life from that time of trial until he became king of the Israelites.

God works to build character in every leader. He uses circumstances, people and situations in any combination to achieve that end.

David was ready to change history when he became king of Israel. He gathered the people and announced that his first act as king would be to bring back the Ark of the Covenant. They all agreed, and left to get the Ark. (You can read the account of this in 1 Chronicles chapters 13, 14, and 15.)

There was one problem: David forgot to ask God about the proper way to carry the Ark of the Covenant. Notice that David knew *what* to do – but he didn't take time to ask God *how* to do it.

David offers a prime example of what happens in the reality stage. David needed not only the knowledge of what to do, but also the knowledge of how to put that knowledge into practice. The method is vital in leadership.

David led the way in bringing the Ark back to Israel on a cart that was pulled by oxen. The people of Israel joined the parade with singing and rejoicing. What a celebration! David was singing and dancing before the Lord with all his might. Then Uzziah, one of the priests who was assisting with the Ark, reached out to support the Ark as it began to fall off the cart. That was a reasonable response to all who saw it. Yet the action completely violated God's law regarding the treatment of the Ark of the Covenant. There was a tragic consequence: God's anger burned against the priest and as punishment, he died.

That event brought David to another part of the reality stage. David was devastated and angry. He questioned God: "Why, Lord? I'm trying to serve you! Why this punishment? Why is this disaster coming upon me? What did I do, Lord?"

David was turning away from his own way of doing things to seek God again. In that process, the Lord reminded David that the Ark of the Covenant was never meant to be moved from place to place by placing it on a cart pulled by oxen. The Word says the priests should consecrate themselves, put on their garments and carry the Ark on their shoulders. That was God's law, and it would not change even due to David's excitement or ideas about what it meant to serve God.

David repented. He admitted he had not sought the Lord the way he needed to. He then directed the priests to consecrate themselves and then bring the Ark of the Covenant to Jerusalem, Israel's capital city.

The reality stage means owning up to weaknesses. It means learning a new level of dependence upon God.

Mulatu Belachew reflects, "The attitude, 'There's a lot I *don't* know,' will take you a long way in facing reality." It also opens up wide horizons for God to build character in a leader, as Mulatu's story will show.

CHARACTER BUILDING ACROSS CULTURES

"God builds character daily. Often I learned that as I was confronted in cross-cultural situations. How did God build that character? Time with Him is the primary element. Yet those lessons had to be exercised in everyday life. In my case, those lessons have come both at work and at home.

"I am approaching three decades of daily cross-cultural involvement professionally. I have been managed by – and managed – a number of different personalities from a wide variety of cultures along the way. The fact that I have been married to my wife Karin, a Swedish national, for over 26 happy years has made me face a great number of cross-cultural issues, too!

"The whole foundation for cross-cultural learning – which today is more vital in building the kingdom of God than ever before – is a solid foundation in God's Word. The Word brings out the failings and strengths common to people everywhere. It pronounces God's intent for every person He created. If those presuppositions of the Word are ingrained in a leader, learning about others is much easier – and more fruitful.

"I don't know that I can point to one big cross-cultural lesson but I can offer a number of daily lessons that have shaped me over the years. Many of them center on a common theme: *Why has God placed us together?*

"The first such incident I can remember happened early in my years with World Vision. I reported to an American vice president of the organization at that time, who became a valuable mentor in helping me put leadership in a cross-cultural perspective. He flew from the States to Nairobi, Kenya, to help me sort through some ideological issues we did not agree upon.

"It is no shame to either of us to say that Americans and Africans see many things differently. We had some serious items to work through before we could successfully work together. We spent two working days together in a locked room. We brought out every possible impasse we could think of that could hinder our partnership. It seemed overwhelming. Surely there was too much between us, between our cultures, between our viewpoints.

"Then he brought it to a close with a simple thought. He closed our second day together with the reminder, 'There's nothing we can do to change many of these things. But, hey, we're stuck together.'

"That said all that needed to be said. Before, our outlook had been 'How many differences do we need to overcome?' After, we learned to focus on 'What can we find in common to build the future?' It was a reminder of life in the body of Christ at its best. What do we have in common? Is a common Lord and a common Kingdom enough?

"What is a viewpoint? It's liberating to remember that a point of view is just that – the view from one point as one person sees it. That means we see things others don't, and others see things we don't. Nobody save God sees it all. We must understand we don't see the whole world, only the view from that point where God has brought us.

"The greatest joy in cross-cultural experience – and in everyday relationships, cross-cultural or not – is the richness in learning from others. Too many leaders are lone rangers. God positions each of us in specific places. We need to perform well in our positions, yet keep in mind that we don't know everything someone else knows."

TRANSITION TOWARD MATURITY: THE REALITY REVIEW

The reality stage is a transition from knowing to practicing. Take a look again at the practical humility in Mulatu's statement that closes the previous section: "We need to perform well in our positions, yet keep in mind that we don't know everything someone else knows."

There is confidence in Mulatu's statement, but not arrogance. He describes the ideal transition in the reality stage very well. It is a movement from "head knowledge" to life application. It's not an issue of being able to perform; it's an issue of showing godly character as you lead. You may be in a leadership role, but you will never replace the guidance of the Holy Spirit with your own talents and experience. It is clearly a transition from building one's own kingdom to building the kingdom of God.

In early success, it's easy for a leader to start building his or her personal kingdom. The challenge for Moses, after bringing Israel out of Egypt, was that it was easy for him to tell them that he knew what it would take to get water for them at Marah. But God said, "No! It's not your knowledge and experiences, it's my guidance and leading that you need."

The reality stage is also a time of progressing from being guided by personal vision to God's vision. It's surrendering to God and saying, "Lord, I see *this*. Is *this* what you see too, Lord?" This is the type of approach to take. It's going from knowing how to do it, to knowing God. It's advancing from knowledge to wisdom.

The reality stage moves one from childish acts into maturity. Reality prepares us to enter the maturity stage, which we'll discuss in the next chapter. The reality stage is very challenging. This is where people encounter a valley. They often experience rejection or a sense of failure. They feel people don't understand or accept them. The question becomes, "How can I change this reality stage into a successful experience?" This is done a number of ways.

First, a leader needs to understand that God requires the reality stage for character building. It's not for destruction. This is why the Bible says, "*And we know that in all things God works for the good of those who love him, who have been called according to his purpose,*" (Romans 8:28). The issue is, *according to His purpose*. If a leader loves the Lord, if he knows he's called according to the purpose of God, then all things will work together for his good. It's a willingness to be *made*, trusting and having faith in God. The reality stage for Paul was in Acts chapter 27 when his ship was broken into pieces. The angel of the Lord came that night, stood by him and said, "Paul, I have given you, not only your life, but the lives of people who are with you in the boat."

As far as circumstances were concerned, this was impossible. The ship was in pieces, after all. Paul got up in the morning and saw the waves still raging, yet Paul told his fellow passengers that none of them would perish. He believed it would happen, just as the Lord told him. It was his faith in operation. Part of character building for any leader should produce a greater trust in God.

Second, the reality stage brings us to a deeper knowledge of God. This is not a question of knowing how to do things, but rather of knowing God Himself. This is why Paul said, "*…I know whom I have believed, and am convinced that he is able to guard what I have entrusted to him for that day,*" (2 Timothy 1:12). Mark those words, "I am convinced." Paul knows God. We are to know Him in the same way. Again,

Stage 4: The Reality Stage

it's not only knowing what we're supposed to do and having leadership skills, but it is truly *knowing God*.

Third, the reality stage makes us aware of our own weaknesses or shortcomings. Through the reality stage, God reveals weak areas that He wants us to bring to Him. He then can cover our weaknesses. His strength will be revealed through our weaknesses.

Fourth, the reality stage helps us recognize our gifts. In early leadership a leader works with untested gifts. The reality stage teaches the leader to really understand where his or her gifts and strengths are. Therefore, it brings each leader into a position of genuine teamwork with others as each one exercises his or her gifts – and looks for help where weakness exists.

Fifth, the reality stage produces a deeper discernment of the calling and purpose of God. With all the challenges this stage presents, knowing why God has called you – and knowing the goal that's set before you – are essential.

Sixth, the reality stage forces a review of God's promises. It's important to go back, at the reality stage, to the promises given at the time of calling. What did God say? How did He call me? What is my foundation? The reality stage enables a leader to check his foundation. Where do I stand? Am I on a solid rock or am I on the sand? Am I grounded?

Seventh, the reality stage calls the leader to depend upon the resources of God. This is the core understanding: "I can't do it, but God can. Yes, I'm limited, but my God isn't!" This kind of knowledge will move us from knowing into believing. I believe in God, the One who has called me. Yes, I see my shortcomings, and where I'm weak, but I can trust in God. This is "believing" faith.

Hebrews 11 deals with this. All leaders who served the Lord came back to this issue of faith, of believing and trusting in God, and standing on His promises. The progression at the reality stage is I know, I believe and I stand. The reality stage, through faith in God, is the reality, power, grace and mercies of God. This brings us to the point where we're able to say, "I know God, I believe in Him and I stand for the purpose He has called me to."

TAKING ON THE CHALLENGES

The reality stage presents a series of challenges. One is trying to create a way out, without depending on God. It's tempting for a leader to try his own creative solution to a problem rather than to turn to God for help. This is dangerous. The leader must ask the Lord for the solution to his dilemma. It's easy to feel overwhelmed by the challenges of the reality stage. The temptation is to repeat a past success instead of asking the Lord for the new work He wants to do through the current circumstances and situation.

There's also the temptation to follow wrong advice. For example, instead of waiting for the Lord to bring his heir into being, Abraham listened to Sarah. Her advice was lacking in both patience and wisdom. She encouraged Abraham to bypass the fact that God had promised a child from her own womb. Sarah told Abraham to take her maidservant and have a child from her. Ishmael arrived, and later on Abraham was distressed due to the conflict over Ishmael. He paid the price because of what he had done. The issue here is, because of the reality or challenge, one listens to wrong advice. A leader must guard against the challenge to take wrong advice.

There is also the challenge of impatience. Joseph tried to plead his way out of prison through a cupbearer who had once shared his cell, instead of waiting for the Lord's timing for his freedom. Saul refused to wait for Samuel to perform a sacrifice to God and lost his credibility before the prophet and God.

Confusion between leadership and management is also a problem at this stage. In the reality stage, the person struggles and wonders if they are to cast a vision and lead, or manage and get involved in day-to-day activities. There is confusion as to how to develop one's role.

Another challenging issue is accountability. Who should the leader trust for an honest assessment? Who prays with the leader for God's guidance regarding the next step? Who understands what the leader goes through? Those answers all hinge around the answer to this question: To whom am I accountable? In early leadership, accountability is rarely a concern. It takes a dose of reality to make it an issue for many leaders on the journey.

Once a person starts struggling with these issues, the way to come out of the valley is by understanding the full purpose of God. Again, the purpose of God is not to destroy, but to build and understand that the One who called the leader is faithful. The verse to stand on is 1 Thessalonians 5:24: *"The one who calls you is faithful and he will do it."* This means trusting in the ability of the Lord, calling on His power and depending on Him. The reality stage is indeed the time to seek the face of the Lord and surrender to His purpose and His will.

LESSONS LEARNED

Mulatu Belachew sought God during the reality stage of his leadership journey. The following reflections come from his experience.

"God doesn't give us territory. God gives us people – and other people have a valid understanding of the world, too.

"God is cross-cultural. He communicates with tribes, with people groups and to nations. That is one key lesson from the reality stage of my own leadership journey. Leadership is not about increasing one's own territory, it is about building the kingdom of God.

"There is also the need to self-evaluate. This discipline should lead to greater confidence in God, and to a greater recognition of the truth that success is a result of God's blessing, far more than a result of your own efforts.

"Self-evaluation also brings with it far greater honesty regarding your strengths, gifts and weaknesses. This is crucial for a leader because this stage demands that you move from merely understanding yourself into practicing what you have learned. And you practice what you have learned not simply to stack up more individual successes, but instead – I will say it again – to build the kingdom of God."

WHERE CAN YOU GO FROM HERE?

Perhaps you find yourself in the reality stage of leadership, or maybe you're just entering this stage. Use this time to discover. Reality should lead you to a fresh discovery of your strengths, your weaknesses, your gifts, your call and into a deeper relationship with God.

God will use this time to build character. That means you should anticipate challenges that will mature you and take you from self-dependence to a new depth of dependence on God.

As a result, your focus will shift from serving your own purposes to building the kingdom of God. If your leadership experience is still more about securing your own territory than submitting yourself to God's objectives, be prepared for more character building.

This stage is structured to bring a leader into fuller maturity – and launch the leader into reaping the benefits of that maturity.

QUESTIONS FOR REFLECTION

1. *Whether or not you believe yourself to be in the reality stage of leadership, think of one specific time where God has used the reality around you to build your character. What did you learn from that experience? How has it helped you as a leader?*
2. *The reality stage is a time of transition. How can transition be difficult for a leader? How can it be a blessing?*

What surprises you more as a leader: discovering a personal strength, or discovering a personal weakness? Why?

Stage 5
The Leadership Journey

I The Call
Process of >Hearing >Discerning >Promise >From, to and for

II Acceptance
Process of >Step of faith >Entering >Commission >Confirmation >Signs

III Early Leadership
Process of >History >Ministry >People >Team

IV Reality
Process of >Character building >Self discovery >Facing reality >Personal gifts >Call >God >Knowledge

V Maturity
Process of >Building Ministry >Recognizing offices >Correcting History >Making History >Shaping History

VI Value Stage
Process of >Relationship >Building people >Becoming a father >Bearing Fruit >Establishing Pattern

VII Relational Stage
Process of >Relationship >Leaving a legacy

V Maturity
Process of
>Building Ministry
>Recognizing offices
>Correcting History
>Making History
>Shaping History

THE MATURITY STAGE

Jesus said to them, "Come and have breakfast."
... Jesus came, took the bread and gave it to them,
and did the same with the fish. (John 21:12, 13)

Experience is not what happens to a man. It is what a man does with what happens to him.

– Aldous Huxley

A mature leader is able to focus on that which is really important. That kind of focus marks this stage in the leadership journey.

During the maturity stage a leader serves in many ways. The leader recognizes his or her unique role in God's kingdom. Mature leaders in the Bible accomplished remarkable things:

- **Joshua** established the people of Israel in the Promised Land, finally correcting their history of rebellion in the wilderness.
- **Ezra** recovered the covenant and rebuilt the Temple.
- **Hezekiah** restored new order to God's people.
- **Paul** took the opportunity to share the Gospel with Roman leaders.

The hand of God is on the mature leader. His favor truly rests on that person. This stage brings the leader to his or her highest level of service. Best of all, as a mature Christian leader serves, he or she reflects the image of Christ.

The journey in this stage is marked by:
- The leader recognizing his or her gift and office
- Recognizing the gifts of others
- Laying a foundation for others to build upon
- Building ministry
- Focusing on the mission and vision of the ministry
- Correcting what is not right
- Starting processes that will shape history
- Making history

Watch for these characteristics as you examine the next two chapters.

Chapter 9

Getting Your Hands Dirty

As we just discussed, in the reality stage God allows challenges in order to build character in the leader. It brings the leader to consider the ultimate call of God: to be conformed to the image of the Lord Jesus Christ. According to Romans 8: 28, Paul says, *"And we know that in all things God works for the good of those who love him, who have been called according to his purpose."* "All things" includes the challenges of the reality stage – because whatever God brings into the life of a leader in the reality stage will lead that individual into the maturity stage.

The maturity stage brings a person, in his personal calling, to the highest level in his walk with the Lord. The call of every Christian leader is to be a reflection of God, and to be conformed into the image of the Lord Jesus Christ. This is the maturity stage. Maturity is not just the ability to do the work well, understand what it takes and be well established. True maturity in leadership comes when a person focuses on being transformed into the image of the Lord Jesus Christ.

In the maturity stage, what God is after is not simply what a person can accomplish through daily or annual plans. A person understands that God is interested in his own personal life and what God can do through him. In the transition from early leadership to the maturity stage, the person's focus changes from what he can accomplish for God, to how much he lets God perform His will and purpose through his life. This means a willingness to let God be God, and to open his heart, mind and soul to the will and purpose of God. This is maturity.

It is the kind of leadership I experienced under Wally Erickson, past president of Compassion International. Wally brought a wealth of experience to the maturity stage of his leadership journey and offered the following reflections on that stage and his life as a leader.

LEADERSHIP MEANS GETTING YOUR HANDS DIRTY

"My first lessons in leadership were in scouting. Scouting taught me to accept the responsibility of looking after others. It emphasized to learn skills not just for yourself, but to help someone else.

"There's no chance in scouting for a leader at any level to say, 'I'm not going to get my hands dirty.' You lead by coming alongside someone and working with them. It's a value I've carried with me all my life.

"I worked as a leader in several scout camps as I grew up. I also worked as a lifeguard – a kind of position that taught me to make quick decisions, and reminded me that those decisions could drastically affect someone else's life.

"In fact, I worked my way through college as a lifeguard and swimming instructor. That experience reaffirmed that leadership often demanded being right alongside those you wanted to lead. There certainly was no way to teach swimming without getting in the water with my students!

"I was wonderfully converted early in my freshman year of college. Everything was new. I'd attended church regularly, but this was different. The Bible took on a new meaning. Prayer took on a new dimension. My emphasis shifted from the outdoors and the water to serving others.

Stage 5: The Maturity Stage

"Just a few months after my conversion, I thought God might be calling me to become a missionary. I thought my outdoor skills could take me to the 'outback' where no one else wanted to go.

"I was still working through how to respond to God's calling when I finished college and began seminary. I took on a job as an inspector for the Bendix Corporation in government contract projects. I was the go-between guy, caught between the government and the manufacturer. God used that to develop more backbone in me. I had to say 'no' to the manufacturer sometimes, and other times I had to stand up to the government buyers. I learned a lot about negotiation during those years, too.

"I took all this experience from a wide variety of exposure into four pastorates. Each pastorate was considered a success by those around me, but I wasn't escaping the feeling that God had something else in mind for me. After the fourth pastorate, I re-evaluated my life. Until that point, I'd allowed circumstances to dictate my course. But then I began a deep search for God's guidance.

"I ended up with just a few points to build upon. God showed me that my best gift was working with young people outside a formal church setting. I certainly enjoyed using my skills as an outdoorsman with them. It was a different approach to leading – a more hands-on, experience-based sort of teaching. But God seemed to say clearly that I could communicate the Gospel message to others by showing it as well as telling it.

"It looked as though I was headed into a different ministry than the traditional pulpit. When I left the pastorate to pursue this vision of hands-on Christian work with children, a lot of my friends called it 'leaving the ministry.'

"But God let me know I wasn't leaving the ministry. Instead, he was redefining it."

MATURITY INTO MINISTRY

After years in the pastorate, Wally Erickson allowed God to show him his unique role in the Kingdom. Without that act of faith, Wally might never have discovered the level of service God intended for him. This submission to God's ideas about what role to take, what office is appropriate – regardless of public recognition or lack of it – demonstrates the heart of a mature leader.

At the maturity stage, a person recognizes not only the calling or purpose of God for his life, but also his office. A person then operates within that position. At the maturity stage, a leader stops competing with others. He also stops trying to be like others. In Wally's case, once he recognized his role was somewhere outside the traditional pastorate, he laid down that office to pursue the office God had for him.

In this stage a leader understands his own personal gifts, but not with a sense of pride. The person accepts his gifts, and knows the Lord has called him to something in the context of the Church or the Kingdom. If God calls him to be an apostle, he isn't ashamed to accept the call. He's ready for whatever God has called him to be. He accepts the call and asks God for help in being faithful to the office he's been called to and maximizing the use of his gift.

Maturity doesn't mean that a person is better than, or less than, others are. God has simply called them to an office. At the maturity stage the person seeks the anointing more than recognition. In early leadership, the focus is on recognition. Who will recognize me? Who will love and accept me? This is a driving force. Because of challenges in the reality stage, God removes burdens that aren't from Him – and also cuts branches that don't bear fruit in the leader's life. This brings a leader to the maturity stage.

When a person reaches this stage, the leader focuses on the anointing and bearing fruit for the Lord. It's no longer important who recognizes him or loves him, but rather that he or she is following God's will. The questions become, "Is God pleased with my life? How am I handling my calling? Am I doing what God has called me to? Where am I?" These questions bring a leader to the maturity stage, just as they brought Wally Erickson to it. Let's continue with Wally's story.

FINDING THE OFFICE

"As God reaffirmed my personal gifts, it became necessary that the parameters of my ministry become more narrowly defined. I had to become more narrowly focused. My vision was refined to ministry with children.

"For several years, my wife Mary and I focused on work with children and youth through camps and conferences. We developed a proposal for work among Native American youth, and presented it to Compassion International. Compassion had no work among the Native Americans at that time, but they did have a place for me.

"The real philosophy of a person is hammered out on the anvil of life. Scouting taught me that real leaders get their hands dirty. Being a lifeguard showed me that others' lives can depend on my actions. The Bendix experience taught me negotiation and the need for attention to detail. The pastorate introduced me to the truth that ministry brings with it both great satisfaction and intense pressure.

"God brought all this experience together for me at Compassion. He showed me how the preparation of the earlier years combined into the leadership role he had for me. I spent four years as the country director of Korea, and several years following opening Compassion's work as the field director for the Caribbean, Central America and South America.

"I was also able to develop and negotiate a new approach for Compassion's ministry – one that focused on a church-related school as the center of program activity. I then took on the role of Executive Vice President of Operations for one year, and was then appointed president of Compassion.

"It still amazes me to think about how wonderfully God prepared me for that unique position. He truly redefined what leadership meant for my life – and it certainly didn't look traditional!"

BEARING FRUIT THROUGH WISDOM

Just as we saw in Wally's story, in the maturity stage a leader brings together a combination of knowledge and wisdom. He has experience from the early leadership and reality stages, but now life experiences and knowledge come together and bring forth wisdom at the highest level. The person learns from this, walks in discernment, and begins to discern what is and isn't important.

A sense of fear or feeling threatened is less common in the maturity stage. Here the leader doesn't mind sharing authority or delegating responsibilities. (In fact, as we'll see in Wally's story, this is often the stage when a leader selects his or her successors.) Maturity not only helps a person recognize his own gifts, abilities and limitations, but he also recognizes the same things in others. He understands the limitations and gifts of individuals. He discerns and is more and more committed to see maturity and gifts in the lives of others.

The leader also recognizes Body life in this stage. He sees the gifts of God in the lives of others. He sees himself as just one individual whom God has called for a special purpose at this time. At the maturity stage a person has a desire to walk with the Lord, do His will, walk in obedience, turn everything over to the Lord and trust in Him. Maturity comes through faith and trust.

We see this in the life of Paul, time and again in his ministry, when he said, "The Lord is with me." He saw that God was with him. He trusted in the ability and protection of the Lord. In the maturity stage, circumstances aren't as important. The focus is on accomplishing the will of God, *whatever the circumstances.* That's why when Paul and Barnabas were imprisoned, they sang. When the Apostles were beaten, they rejoiced. Their focus wasn't on their circumstances, but rather on accomplishing the purposes and call of God.

Maturity is when a leader's focus is on accomplishing the purpose and will of God. This is extremely important. The major focus for a person in the maturity stage is not building one's personal reputation, popularity, or their personal kingdom. In true maturity a person focuses on the kingdom of God and building God's kingdom.

At this stage, seeing and hearing what God is doing is critically important for a leader. A leader is striving and longing to see what God sees and to hear what God is saying. One of the characteristics of mature spiritual leaders is to know the heart of the Father. "What is on God's heart? Yes, I'm in a ministry. Yes, I'm accomplishing a lot, but what's on the heart of my Father?"

This is why the Lord Jesus spent so much time in prayer. Jesus' consistent and dedicated prayer life gave Him the confidence to say something every leader should be able to say: "I don't do anything that I haven't seen the Father doing. I do only what I've seen the Father doing" (see John 8:28).

It comes down to this: At the maturity stage, mere activities don't satisfy a spiritual leader. Just accomplishing an agenda is not satisfying to him. In early leadership, accomplishment is a big thing. "I've done this much . . . I've written so many books . . . I've done this and that . . ." All the accomplishments and lists of activities are important to the early leader. In the maturity stage, the issue isn't how much, but rather, what does God want? What does God want me to do and how well am I doing it? The foundation is very important. How *well* something is done is more important at this stage than how *much*.

Pursuing the "how well" approach leads a person into a true understanding of the heart of God, the heart of the Father. It helps the leader better discern the mind of Christ. The ministry must be carried out with humility to serve and accomplish the will of God. The maturity stage brings consistency in leadership style and character. This reduces the valley that was part of life in early leadership.

In early leadership, the focus is on power and the ability to control. At the maturity stage, there's also focus on power, but not personal power. Rather, it's on the power of the Holy Spirit. One needs to depend on the power of the Holy Spirit. "I can do all things through Christ Jesus" becomes the focus in the mature leader's life. Because of this, keeping and protecting the anointing given by God becomes very important. The maturity stage further distinguishes the agenda of the Kingdom from a leader's personal agenda.

A leader at this stage of the journey isn't as concerned with time. Unlike Saul, the mature leader doesn't jump into making a sacrifice. Rather, a person is willing to wait upon the Lord, to follow His timetable instead of a personal timetable.

The maturity stage also leads a person into the method. A person not only seeks what to do, but also asks the Lord how to do it. *Lord, how do you want us to do this? Yes, we have done this before and I know how others are doing it, but I want to ask you.*

This is characteristic of the maturity stage. This is what David did. As he became a strong king and started conquering more, because of David's maturity, his relationship with God and his desire, he always asked God how to go to war. The question, *Lord, what do you want us to do?* marked the basis of any success David had.

The mature leader also will not have a problem recognizing the call of others. In fact, he or she will start encouraging others who have a similar or related calling, and is comfortable with it. Paul, in a more immature stage, wasn't willing to take Mark or anyone else with him as he built the Early Church. Later on, Paul matured and said he needed Timothy with him and wanted the support. At the value stage, the discipleship issue comes in, but the fatherly caring and ability to discern others' gifts emerges in the maturity stage. The calling or character of others doesn't intimidate a mature person. He knows his own gift and recognizes others' gifts. In fact, he tries to maximize others' gifts in areas where he lacks gifts.

Wally Erickson lived out these truths of a mature leader as he sought to select his successor. We'll pick up Wally's story as he begins that process.

NO INTIMIDATION, JUST A BRIGHTER FUTURE

"A lot of people have asked me when I really came to recognize that I was going to need someone to follow me. I can honestly tell you that it wasn't so much a planned effort, as it was almost a lightning bolt from heaven. I met Wess Stafford and had become familiar with him while he was in Haiti. I watched the way he dealt with the people of Haiti. I was cognizant of some of his philosophy and background of how he had a great heart of love for people of developing nations such as Haiti.

"I invited Wess to speak in Compassion's chapel when he was in Chicago shortly after we'd met. God began putting things together for me – how I'd seen Wess work in Haiti, his message that morning, all I'd heard about him. I went home after chapel and said to my wife Mary, 'I've found the next president of Compassion International.'

"It wasn't that I needed to be busy looking for this person, but here was a potential candidate. Here was a person who had a heart. Wess has a great passion and heart of loving people. I think that's because of what God placed in his life: his background, parents, missionary involvement and education. The more I found out about him, the more I thought there was an awful lot to build on. So in my case, I had a secret in my heart for a long time that he might be the one.

"Since I found someone I thought might be my successor, I then started to look for other candidates. I felt that it was my responsibility to give the board as many options as possible. So I started looking for other possibilities within and without Compassion. I looked for skills, gifts and professional qualifications, but mostly I looked for heart. More than anything else, I wanted to know if their heart could be broken; if their heart really bled for the kind of work that we're doing.

"In my opinion, you may find 20 or 30 Ph.D.s who are well-trained individuals. But I'm not sure they would all have a heart for the work that is Compassion. You know, the hardest job we have is to live up to our name. So unless there's someone at the head of Compassion who exemplifies compassion in his heart, life, attitudes and dealings with people, then everything else is only a farce. The mission of the ministry and the heart of the person have to mesh. I saw that in Wess.

"Wess would shape the organization for years if he was God's person for the job. I felt it was important, then, to invest in Wess. I actually made a deal with Wess that he should go on to get his Ph.D. We would subsidize some of his schooling for the time it took him to finish. In exchange, he would come back and serve us for the same period of time, and write his dissertation about something relevant to child development. Wess agreed to those terms.

"That was part of his preparation. I think you need to invest in young people that you think have potential. We were willing to invest in Wess: time, education, and training. We invested by sending him back to Haiti to do his field work for his dissertation. We invested in him to get the dissertation written and then to defend it. That took time. It took time away from his responsibilities here. But the investment put me in a position to help him be accountable for finishing his doctorate.

"As the years went on, I took the opportunities I could to be a mentor to Wess. That means Wess and I had lots of conversations, not just in this office, but wherever we went – as we traveled and when we hunted together. We tried to keep business out of pleasure, but at the same time, it was always time to dialogue and explore the depths of the other person. You talk about the person having to reconfirm his call, about his understanding of what God wants him to do, about what he believes. As we go through life we start sorting things out. Even though we may go to seminary or get a Ph.D., we have to put everything to the test in our lives.

"Sometimes when people see leadership, right away they think it's the guy at the top. No, it can be a man at any place and at every level. There's a unique kind of leadership for each need. It may be a dozen people fitting together very neatly, each doing his unique gift, but together becoming the ministry that God wants to accomplish.

"I think one of the real characteristics of leadership is to recognize as you become narrowly focused and discover your own personal gifts from God, that, 'Wow, this is more than I can possibly do. This needs far more than I am.' When this happens, what do you do?

"You start to gather other people around you who have those particular gifts needed for that particular task. In fact, you need to bring in people who are probably more gifted than yourself in many different areas. That's part of God's plan. When you're mature, you're not threatened by other people. You won't be threatened if you see that their task is going to be different than yours. But if you think that they're going to be exactly like you, then all of a sudden they're a real threat. I think you need to see them in God's eyes and in God's plan and purpose. Then they are all unique. Look for people, basically, who have all the things that you don't have. Together you complement each other.

"That's what's so beautiful about marriage. Whoever said a male and female are exactly alike? They're not. They're meant to complement each other. God looked at Adam and said, 'This is not good. You have to have someone to be a helpmate.' In much the same way, a leader might consider a situation and say, 'This is not good. I can't do this by myself. I need a lot of helpmates.' So you start looking for people who do things that you can't.

"I really don't like to speak in front of large groups. So for many years I used Wess in one of his greatest gifts: communication. When I got an invitation to tell a group about

Compassion I'd say, 'Wess, here! I've got a job for you!' I'd send him out, because that's his gift! I was thrilled to let him do it! Can you imagine the joy I've received in watching him use and develop those gifts for Compassion and God's kingdom?

"A leader must have a sense of joy in the success of others around you being used of God. You can't feel that somehow the success of God's mission throughout the world rests on your shoulders in leadership. No. It rests on lots of people. You need them. They're not there to intimidate you. With them, you could well build a better future."

Chapter 10

Setting the Example – Under Authority

In the role to which God has called him, the mature individual not only accomplishes the work, but also sets an example. In this stage, a life example is very important. His life should exemplify what he does by the way he lives. If a leader offers a sound example to others, they feel more compelled to follow.

The leader's example should demonstrate his or her personal devotion to Christ in this stage. A leader should be able to say, just as Paul said, "Follow me as I follow Christ." The focus is on Christ at the maturity stage. Mature leaders don't spend time trying to hide their weaknesses. Rather, they admit their weaknesses and bring them to the Lord.

The maturity stage is a process. It's moving from glory to glory. It doesn't stop at one point. In this process, the maturity stage is usually a mark of the ministry and at the centrality of it. Not in the sense of depending on how much a person serves the Lord before or after, but as far as the actual *accomplishments* are concerned. It's the "mid-term" of the leadership journey. Some people take a long time to reach the maturity stage. Others come to the mid-term earlier. Whatever the timing, once a person reaches the maturity stage, the most crucial ministry is what's coming, not what has passed. What comes after the maturity stage is more crucial, in that it brings forth the impact of life-changing things in the personal life, by letting God be God. A person is relaxed and available to God, accomplishing and discerning what is and isn't important.

Consider Jesus' example of leadership at the Mount of Transfiguration. This was the mid-term of Jesus' public ministry. For the first time, the disciples who went with Jesus to the Mount of Transfiguration saw Jesus' divinity. They saw His purity, holiness and majesty as He was talking with Moses and Elijah on the mountain. When they saw this they said, "Let's build a tent and dwell here."

Here is a crucial fact: At the maturity stage a leader doesn't forget his purpose. Jesus refused Peter's suggestion to build a tent for Jesus, and one for Elijah. Then the voice of God came as a testimony from heaven after the clouds covered them. The Father said, *"This is my beloved Son; listen to him,"* (Matthew 17:5). At the maturity stage, God doesn't necessarily add activities to a person's agenda, but instead more authority.

In modern leadership, activities and authority are often confused. Success means an increase in activity, as well as increased salary, status or a title. These aren't problems in themselves. However, we have to take into account that in the middle of the ministry of the Lord Jesus Christ, the Father didn't increase Jesus' activities, but rather His authority. Divine authority was increased. "This is my beloved Son" was the same phrase stated at Jesus' baptism. What is added here is, "Listen to him." The difference is in the authority.

At the maturity stage, a leader
- walks with the Lord,
- seeks and is committed to Him,
- puts aside his or her own personal agenda, and
- concentrates on the Kingdom agenda and the will of God.

Then God is the one who brings the testimony and increases the authority. This is another reality of the maturity stage. A person is content with the testimony of God. If God says so, it's enough for me. If God approves it, it's enough for me. It's not an issue of the majority at this stage. It's an issue with the Lord. What is God saying? That's the issue.

At the maturity stage a leader doesn't run around and try to do everything. Moses said to his servant Joshua, "You go fight and I'll go to the mountain and pray." While Joshua was fighting the enemy in battle, Moses raised his hand and prayed. That was his job. Wielding swords and organizing troops was Joshua's task. Moses was praying on top of the mountain. That's the maturity stage in action: *giving responsibility to people according to what they are called to.* The mature leader focuses on what he is responsible for.

Leaders make time to spend with the Lord at this stage. A leader who says he's too busy to spend time with the Lord and seek the face of God, indicates immaturity. In fact, when a leader reaches the maturity level he or she isn't afraid to put things on hold – or to drop them altogether – to seek the face of the Lord. From Moses taking forty days in the midst of the wilderness to go be with God to Jesus removing himself from His ministry schedule, leaders in the Bible did just that.

This is where maturity leads. In the maturity stage it's not only what we do, not the activity, but what we receive from the Lord to pass on to future generations. This is another element of the maturity stage. We see Moses doing this as he received the word or instruction of the Lord on the mountain. He could then go back and say, "My brothers, here it is. Here is guidance from the Lord. This is how you should live and act."

The maturity stage involves setting a pattern and showing the way. The mature leader helps people understand and walk in this, and accomplish the will of the Father through the process.

That's why Wally Erickson made his example clear to those he led, as we're about to find out.

AN EXAMPLE UNDER AUTHORITY

"I think there are different kinds of qualities in others that you look for along the way and try to nurture and encourage. But those who follow you are watching you. Obviously, a leader ought to try - we all have weaknesses - but you need to try your very, very best to be an example of everything you're trying to get the people under you to be. People won't strive to be any more than you are, so there have to be the values of integrity and forthrightness; the value system in your life putting the right priorities in the right area.

"I don't think that you ever look at somebody and think, 'Wow, this person is tailor made for leadership.' I think you look at them and say, 'They have potential.' And God may affirm in your heart that there's potential there, but you have to look at someone at the beginning of what he can be. I think that's the way the Lord deals with us when He saves us. It's what we can be. It has nothing to do with what we are at that moment in time. It begins a process of development. So I think in leadership you need to constantly think about what someone can become, not what he or she is at present. That means you must be an encourager. You must encourage people all along the way.

"It can be like being a father. I like that element, because that certainly is very biblical. Jesus said, 'I say nothing other than what my Father tells me to say. I do nothing other than what the Father tells me to do. Therefore I am under authority, the authority of my Father.' Jesus, I think, was ever conscious that He was under the authority of His Father.

"I think every person needs to be under authority. The model is already there and is set. I think that's another test of leadership. It isn't just 'Can you put other people under your authority?' but, 'Can you keep yourself under authority?' There are two aspects to that. We need to be under the authority of our heavenly Father and we must demonstrate humility as part of that process as an example to others.

"I truly believe that if you can't be under authority you can't be a leader. I really feel that very strongly."

DEVELOPING PERSISTENCE FOR GOD'S VISION

In today's society, the greatest problem in the maturity stage of leadership is ignoring one's own need to be under authority. A second problem is lack of understanding the purpose for doing things. For whose sake are we doing this? Was it for appearance's sake or in obedience to God?

Here is where maturity comes in. At the maturity stage, a leader doesn't care how others might respond to his actions if he's done it for the Lord. He just wants to fulfill God's vision. Today, fighting for recognition is a problem with many leaders, Christian and not. Leaders are printing brochures, newsletters and advertising. They want recognition. Leaders are fighting for the platform, to become known. This is not maturity. Leaders think they're at the maturity stage, but behaving this way becomes a challenge for today's Christian leaders.

Leaders, even among evangelicals, also magnify one another more than Jesus. Yet when we reject false honor;

honor at the expense of the kingdom of God, glory of God, purpose of God and what God has called one to, God puts His hand on us. That's when the hand of God comes upon a leader. In the coming years, when mature leaders are committed to God's will, they will even outrun the most powerful political and intellectual leaders – just as Elijah outran Ahab's chariot.

Let's take a closer look at the example of Elijah. At the maturity stage, a leader enjoys God's blessing. One of the characteristics of maturity is fruitfulness. The maturity stage enables a person to bear lasting fruit. In this process a person also understands the promises of God. What are the promises of God for the people, ministry and church or organization I lead, and for my own family? A leader at the maturity stage focuses on the promises of God more than what he can accomplish through his own power and strength. He brings the promises of God to fulfillment, and through this comes God's blessing.

As he struggled against the evil of Ahab and Jezebel in his time of early leadership, Elijah prayed and asked the Lord if God was willing to stop the rain over the land of Israel. God accepted his prayer and gave him permission to speak to King Ahab. He went to the king and said, "Unless I speak a word, there will not be a drop of rain." God accepted this, but Elijah went through a process. He had to hide, drink from a brook and be fed by a bird. This wilderness time wasn't easy, but Elijah was mature enough to fulfill the purpose of God and do what God wanted him to. He was willing to go through the process.

The Lord later told him to go to a widow and God would feed him at the widow's house. He followed these directions. He was willing to go to the widow's house, and God prepared the widow as he prepared the raven: Elijah stayed with her and she fed him. At this point he started bringing God's blessings to the widow. It wasn't only the blessing of having enough to eat through years of drought; it also became a blessing of life itself.

When the widow's only son died, Elijah told her to bring him her dead son. He took the dead child from the woman and went before the Lord. He stretched himself over the child three times and cried to the Lord, asking for the promises of God. He identified with the problem.

A leader in the maturity stage identifies with the problem. He doesn't say the problem is with the department or a person. A true leader identifies with the problem. Because of his maturity, he knows where to take it. Elijah took the child to the Lord. He took the child to the upper room, stretched himself over the child and cried to the Lord. The prophet told God he wanted life for the child as promised by God. God heard his cry and returned life to the boy. The boy became alive.

After this the Lord told Elijah, "Go and reveal yourself to the king. I am going to bring the rain." In the maturity stage God sends a leader out to reveal himself, so the purpose and promises of God can be fulfilled. In early leadership, unlike Elijah in the maturity stage, there's an eagerness to be seen. At the maturity stage, a leader waits for the Lord to tell him when to go to reveal himself.

When Elijah obeyed and revealed himself to the king, he challenged the king by saying the drought was due to the king's disobedience. At the maturity stage a leader has no fear when he's sent for God's purpose. A leader knows his authority. He knows what he's to do. He corrects the problem. Elijah commanded the king to bring the idol worshippers together to show the strength – or lack of it – of their god in contrast to the Lord God. In the maturity stage, a leader who waits upon the Lord and goes according to the Word and timing of God has favor and authority. The king obeyed the prophet and brought all the idol worshippers together.

In the maturity stage, a leader must deal with idols or with what hinders the blessing, whether in a ministry, church or home. A leader is willing to deal with a curse that hinders the blessing God intended for His people. That's what Elijah did. He dealt with idol worship. In the process, he repaired the altar of the Lord. There was renewal and renewed commitment to the one true God of Israel. Repairing the altar of the Lord brought Israel back to the God who deserved their adoration, worship and praises. Elijah repaired the altar of the Lord. The Bible tells us he did it according to the Word of God. After this, he didn't try to help God.

The contest between God and Ba'al that day was a contest to see which deity would be able to send fire to the specific altar dedicated to them. Not only did Elijah *not* try to "help God" in this contest, he directed that a ditch be dug around the altar and then filled with water. One of the characteristics of early leadership is trying to help God. One tries to do everything to help God. The maturity stage brings a person to where he doesn't make an effort to help God, but rather trusts in the power of God. He does things according to God's purpose and plan. The distinction between early leadership and the maturity stage is that in early leadership an individual tries to prove and do things their own way. In the maturity stage the person follows God's will and obeys God, but doesn't try to help God accomplish something.

After preparing everything, Elijah prayed for the fire of God to come down – and God answered. When the fire of God came, there was a cleansing. There's cleansing when God's fire comes. In the maturity stage, idols are removed and there's cleansing: Purity of character and life results.

One last thing: At the maturity stage, a leader does not stop because of his initial success. He continues on. A problem in early leadership is that after his first success, the leader is tempted to stop. At the maturity stage, a leader will not stop until he sees the total fulfillment of God's purpose. In Elijah's case, that meant he went to the king and said he heard the sound of heavy rain. He said to go down and get ready, eat and drink, as rain was coming. He told this to the king. There had been no rain for three and one-half years, but he took a step of faith. The purpose was to show the king once and for all that God alone controlled the welfare and history of Israel.

The maturity stage is characterized by faith or trust in God, and standing on the promises of God. The leader does things according to the purpose of God, but believes and trusts God for the fulfillment. In 1 Kings 18, when Elijah heard the sound of heavy rain, he didn't see anything on earth, but referred to what was still in the heavens. It was still to be revealed. At the maturity stage, a leader looks beyond what's around him or the circumstances, and instead draws from the promises of God. Unless a leader knows in his heart what God has for the people he leads, he can not make it become a reality. The mature leader accepts and possesses the purposes of God, and has the ability to see what God is doing. Elijah was in tune with the things of God.

It is one thing to receive the promises of God, but it's an even bigger step to stand on the promises of God and ask God to fulfill those promises. Elijah already saw a great rain in the heavens, but he still had to pray to see the reality of rain on earth. Sometimes leaders receive the promises of God, but don't ask, pray or go to the Lord and plead with Him for an answer. If God promises it, then it's up to the leader to pray through to receive the promise. Elijah prayed until he saw the actual thing – and it happened.

A CLEARER VISION

Elijah's example should not be considered as uncommon for the mature leader. In fact, the spiritual vision of a leader becomes clearer in maturity.

It's popular for leaders to talk about vision these days, but far more difficult for any of us to take a truthful look at the sort of vision we have. Yet that is crucial for maturity in leadership.

Why? Some leaders actually lack vision. They are unable to look at future possibilities because they remain bound to the past. When asked about their vision, they tend to talk about past policies and experiences rather than the potential for God's work in the future. Their common response to change is, "We've never done it this way before."

Other leaders have an unformed vision. They see no boundary between God's vision for their leadership role and their own desires. The result is that they mix their own desires in with God's purposes, producing a vision that is very difficult to define for others. Yet these leaders tend to call their unformed visions God-given, which makes them very difficult to work with. They cannot see the difference between what God has in store for them and what they have always wanted anyway – and neither can those who follow them.

Still other leaders have a scattered vision. They see parts of God's vision for them clearly, but tend to jump from one part to another without finishing what they started. They do not create any kind of continuity in their actions. As the pattern repeats, it becomes difficult for their followers to take them very seriously.

Another kind of challenge presents itself when a leader has a disorganized vision. They see clearly, but don't understand God's timing and sequence. They have no idea what to address first in the vision, and as a result often violate God's timing of events.

Insecure leaders tend to have limited vision. These leaders are usually fine administrators and visionaries, yet their own insecurity limits the breadth of how God's vision would otherwise apply to their situation. This results in their needlessly limiting the gifts and callings of others whose activity looks "too risky."

A leader can be too confident, on the other hand, and end up with a completely ego-driven vision. These leaders are intelligent visionaries, effective implementers, and "corporate climbers." Yet their very success convinces them that they should become the focus of the organization at the expense of Kingdom-building.

The goal, of course, is for the leader to develop a healthy vision. The focus of this vision is God and His purposes. No person can be qualified as a leader without the promise of true vision. Ministry vision begins with God. Seeing God more clearly will certainly produce a greater clarity in the vision a leader sees for his or her own role and mission – and starting with a vision of the Lord, rather than a vision of activity is one way a leader can keep true focus.

Leaders must also learn to see with God's eyes. This is the foundation of a true leader: to request, then to take on, God's vision for a person, a situation or an organization. This vision should become the basis of strategic planning. It gives leaders both a clear mission and goals as they respond to God's purpose – as He sees it – in their own spheres of influence.

Vision rarely comes in great detail at first. In fact, details only show themselves as the leader walks through the process of leadership in faith and obedience – and in the constant seeking of God.

That kind of dedication certainly produced God-honoring results in Wally Erickson's life as a leader – and it can in yours, too.

LESSONS LEARNED

Wally Erickson was consistent as a mature leader of Compassion International. What would he say he learned during this stage of his leadership journey? The value of focus.

"If God is calling you to leadership, I don't believe that's a nebulous kind of calling. You may begin with broad brushstrokes: 'I want to serve God. I want to be His missionary, His business executive, or whatever.' But I think as we move through life, that calling becomes more focused. It may be applied in several different places of service at different times in your career, but I think it needs to be more narrowly defined as you go.

"As you discover your personal gifts that God has empowered you with, then the parameters of your ministry become more narrowly defined. So you become more narrowly focused. You know better who you are and what it is that God wants you to do. If you don't receive that focus, you aren't going to accomplish much. You'll never be in one situation long enough to mature without definition.

"Everyone has their own focus, too. That's the beauty of teamwork, and in forming a team. Focus has to be a characteristic of a maturing leader; otherwise you're going in all directions: all for good reasons and all because there are needs. But it may not be what God has gifted us as individuals, or as a ministry, or as a business, to do. As we move along, we've got to be able to define our calling and stay focused.

"Good people are capable of getting us off track. Good reasons and good decisions will get us off track. Good rational processes get us off track. A leader must develop the ability to say, 'That's good, but it's not what God wants me to do. That's good, but it doesn't fit my gifts. That's good, but God must have someone else to do that chore. It's not for me.

"So I think as you move through these stages of leadership, there has to be a defining and a narrowing of your focus and vision as to who you are, what God gifted you for and what you want to do. If we are narrowly defined and gifted, and if we really understand gifts, then there is something unique for each one to do. It doesn't mean that your task is better than mine or mine is better than yours, even though it might be a higher place of leadership. It only means God wants me to use my gifts in this particular location."

WHERE DO YOU GO FROM HERE?

In summary, the maturity stage is characterized by focusing on what is really important. In everything leaders do in the maturity stage they ask, "What's important here? Why are we doing this? How should we do it?" If you find yourself focusing on things that have little meaning to the work God has called you to do, you might have to go through more maturing.

A mature leader is looking for something that lasts. At the maturity stage a person begins looking at the impact more than the activity, accomplishment or popularity. He puts these aside and instead focuses on permanent or eternal things. At the maturity stage a person makes distinctions between temporary and eternal matters, as well as those things that are popular versus those that have lasting impact.

In early leadership, a person can find it satisfying to just look at the big green tree. "Look at the tree we've planted. It's growing. Its leaves and branches look fantastic!" At the maturity stage, a leader looks for the fruit. They can look at the tree, but it's not satisfactory. It's just as Jesus said. He looked for the fruit. In John 15:16, the Lord said, *"I have appointed you to bear fruit that lasts."* That is the maturity stage. The person looks at fruit that will last. As you mature as a leader, self-evaluation to find out what kind of fruit you bear is crucial.

Another characteristic of the maturity stage is that a leader is not afraid to pay the price for what's eternal. He's willing to pay the price for the right things. The Apostles paid the price for preaching the Gospel and carrying out the message of the Lord Jesus. They weren't afraid to face all the challenges before them or even death. Jesus did the same thing. He wasn't afraid of rejection. What they did or didn't say didn't move Him. He simply obeyed what God revealed to Him. This is a sign of the maturity stage. If you find yourself struggling with what others think of you, think of the greater value of obedience to God's revelation.

Before the value stage, a person makes a clear distinction between spiritual gifts and love. At the early leadership stage the focus is on spiritual gifts. At the maturity stage, the person focuses on love. This is what Paul said in 1 Corinthians 12-13. Chapter 12 describes the different gifts, but then in 12:31 Paul turns around and says, *"Eagerly desire the greatest gift. Now I'll show you the most excellent way."*

What is the most excellent way of doing things? With biblical love. This is maturity. Maturity will move a person to the excellent way of doing the things of the Lord. Everything must be done in the context of love: love for God, love for people we serve, love for the lost, and love for the cause of the Lord Jesus Christ. And this must be a *true* love. Everything a person does at this stage is motivated by love. This is the highest level of maturity. Paul identifies some of the characteristics of love, which show the maturity of a leader.

In a mature leader, love is patient. Love is kind. It does not envy. It does not boast through accomplishment. It is not proud or rude. It is not self-seeking.

This is the key. Self-seeking is one of the manifestations in early leadership. But at the maturity stage, love takes over and self-seeking stops.

Love is not easily angered. The focus is not on personal issues, but rather on Kingdom issues. The person is not easily angered. He keeps no record of wrongs. The person is more interested in discipling others and bringing the best out of them, rather than just counting wrongs done to him.

Love does not delight in evil, but rejoices in the truth. The mature leader rejoices in what he sees in young leaders.

Love also always protects, trusts and hopes. Here is the patience that's required to train or equip others and to bring or usher them in.

Love always serves. This is maturity. Love brings a person to this stage.

Love is a practical issue today. God is love. As His people, we are called to walk in love. If you lead in self-sacrificing love, you are already maturing. Maturity brings a leader to this point and beyond to the next stage of leadership: the value stage.

Stage 5: The Maturity Stage

QUESTIONS FOR REFLECTION

1. *If you have yet to reach the maturity stage in the leadership journey: What do you most look forward to in this stage? If you have already reached it: What do you enjoy most about this stage?*
2. *"Correcting history" is an important part of the maturity stage. Explain that concept in your own words. What do you see around you – in your own spheres of influence – that God might call you to correct?*

When challenged by someone, what do you do to help bring out the best in them? What might you do to improve your skills in this area?

Stage 6
The Leadership Journey

I The Call
Process of >Hearing >Discerning >Promise >From, to and for

II Acceptance
Process of >Step of faith >Entering >Commission >Confirmation >Signs

III Early Leadership
Process of >History >Ministry >People >Team

IV Reality
Process of >Character building >Self discovery >Facing reality >Personal gifts >Call >God >Knowledge

V Maturity
Process of >Building Ministry >Recognizing offices >Correcting History >Making History >Shaping History

VI Value Stage
Process of >Relationship >Building people >Becoming a father >Bearing Fruit >Establishing Pattern

VII Relational Stage
Process of >Relationship >Leaving a legacy

VI Value Stage
Process of
>Relationship
>Building people
>Becoming a father
>Bearing Fruit
>Establishing Pattern

THE VALUE STAGE

"...I know whom I have believed, and am convinced that he is able to guard what I have entrusted to him for that day"
(2 Timothy 1:12)

Try not to become a man of success, but rather a man of value.
— Albert Einstein

The focus of the value stage is the shaping of history.

Leaders shape history by preparing others to carry on with their mission. This involves modeling leadership to emerging leaders, being an example of one who has a sound relationship with God and communicating the values — through word and deed — that have, and will, provide a foundation for the work God has entrusted to you.

At this stage the leader is comfortable where God has called him or her to serve. The leader will do what is necessary to complete the work God brings to bear in that situation. Leadership is demonstrated through the way the leader handles responsibility. It is also evident in the fruit of his or her service. It is especially shown in relationships, particularly those relationships of mentoring younger leaders.

The goal of a leader in this stage is to help others become all God has intended them to be. The value stage is characterized by:
- Reflection on the past
- Working with clearer vision and purpose
- Building people
- Building relationships
- Focus on releasing the gifts of others

- Mentoring
- Providing coverage while others grow
- Demonstrating the fruits of the Spirit
- Shaping history

Take note of these themes as you read through chapters eleven and twelve.

Chapter 11

Shaping History

The focus of the value stage in the leadership journey is to shape history. The leader in this stage accomplishes this task by
- Reflecting on the past,
- Evaluating the process, and
- Making adjustments to shape history.

Usually this stage is reserved for leaders entering the twilight of their careers. But in the case of Dr. Wess Stafford, who took over the reins of Compassion International at the age of 44, the value stage came early. Wess tells his story as follows.

"I owe a huge debt to the way Wally Erickson mentored me. Wally did everything he could to prepare me to be his successor at Compassion. And honestly, when I first stepped into Compassion's presidency, I thought I was prepared to take the organization to the next level God had for it.

"But then God confronted me with some leadership issues early on. I was alone on a Colorado ranch, taking a break from the office to hunt antelope. I waited out the afternoon until the sun began to set behind the mountains.

"That sunset totally took my mind away from the antelope and into worship. I knelt right there and began to praise God.

"I was overwhelmed that God would take me into a role of leadership like the one at Compassion. I began to think about the children we served – some 150,000 at that time, and another half-a-million through Compassion's program before I became president. I drifted into some mental math. Even with incremental growth, it was likely we'd break the 1,000,000 mark of sponsored children sometime during my tenure. I was thanking God for such a landmark, and the privilege of being part of it, when a voice came over me.

"'That's *all*?' the voice said. 'Well, yes,' I thought. Then the voice delivered this question: 'What about the rest?'

"I realized then that God was calling me to a different kind of leadership to meet both the challenges and potential of a new time. Efforts to 'incrementally help' children wouldn't be enough. I don't think God was calling a particular 'number goal' to my attention, either. But He was calling me to shape history for a new generation of children – and reminding me that business as usual wasn't going to make the grade.

"God began to force me to take a hard look at values. What values had built Compassion? What values would see us through our present challenges? Upon what values could we shape the future?"

God was leading Wess into the value stage of the leadership journey.

MAKING THE MINISTRY MORE PRODUCTIVE

The value stage is an evaluative stage, or a time of reflection. In the value stage, a leader stops and reflects on the past and evaluates the processes, then makes a conclusion about the past for the purpose of making adjustments in the final stage.

It takes maturity to do this. At the maturity stage a person feels comfortable focusing on the kingdom of God. In the value stage, a leader not only corrects what he's been doing or focusing on, but also takes time to correct what went wrong in the past.

The value stage is a unique combination of the past, present and future. The person reflects on and evaluates the past and looks at the reality of where he is today, along with what is happening in this context. They look beyond and into the future, asking, "How can we make the next stage more productive?"

That's exactly what Wess Stafford was doing early in his role as president of Compassion International. So understand this: To say a person has reached the value stage doesn't mean he attains it at 60 years of age or five years before retirement. These aren't the defining factors. Some reach the final or value stage early in life because of the way they handle their responsibilities. Some reach the value stage too late. However, when leaders reach the value stage, they look to the future and bring the reality of past history into context with what is happening now. It's a time for preparing and looking into the future.

Some of the factors that stand out in the value stage are as follows.

FRUIT OF THE SPIRIT

At this stage, a person focuses on the fruit of the Spirit within himself. We know the fruit of the Spirit as listed in Galatians 5:22, *"But the fruit of the Spirit is love, joy, peace, patience, kindness, goodness, faithfulness, gentleness, and self control. Against such things, there is no law."*

In the value stage, the fruit of the Spirit is what characterizes one's personal walk with the Lord, his ministry and his relationship with others. The fruit of the Spirit is obvious in this person's life. It guides everything the leader does.

He evaluates his ministry, life, relationship and walk with the Lord in light of the fruit of the Spirit. The leader will ask, "Am I walking in love? Am I enjoying what I'm doing? Am I at peace? Am I patient? Am I kind and good?"

In fact, the fruit of the Spirit has developed and defined the values that are important to the leader in this stage. That means the ministry that engages the leader, the vision of the ministry and the mission of the ministry are controlled, guided and protected by the fruit of the Spirit. Ministry activity isn't carried out at the expense of the fruit of the Spirit.

This is what's obviously seen in the life and ministry of the Lord Jesus Christ. It's also what we see in the life of Paul towards the end of his ministry. Particularly, this is what we see in the life of those mature leaders who have exemplary lives and ministries. The life of Moses, at the value stage, was characterized by meekness: "*Now Moses was a very humble man, more humble than anyone else on the face of the earth*," (Numbers 12:3).

RELATIONSHIPS

A leader at this stage of the journey values relationships more than anything else: more than accomplishments, successes, possessions, popularity, material gain, or fame.

Relationships become very important to a leader in this stage – beginning with his relationship with God. Indeed, his relationship with God is first. This is where the leader's true passion for God comes in; a passion for the Cross, biblical relationships with others and a desire to walk with God. In fact, at this stage passion and love for God drive a person. A person chooses to run *to* God, rather than running *for* God at this stage. There is a desire to know God and to be in His presence.

David is well known for this through his worship, songs and psalms. His desire and longing is to be with the Lord – to praise and worship Him and to maintain that relationship. Even when he sinned David didn't say, "Lord, please don't take away the kingdom from me." Remember, David saw firsthand what God did with Saul, the first king. Yet David said, "God, don't take away your Spirit from me. Restore to me the joy of my salvation!" David understood the value of his relationship with God, and he didn't want to sacrifice it for anything else.

Throughout His ministry, the number one thing for the Lord Jesus was His relationship with the Father. It was ongoing. Jesus' prayer life, what He said about His Father and the way He worked with His Father demonstrated the importance of the Father in Jesus' life.

That value of increasing one's passion for God was passed on to the Apostles. They showed their dependence upon the Lord – and independence from activity that could be delegated to others – when Peter said, *"Brothers, select from among you those who will serve at the table. We will be diligent in prayer and preaching the gospel,"* (Acts 6:4). It was as though the Apostles agreed, "The focus is on keeping the relationship. We don't want to be too busy serving at the table so we won't have time for prayer. Jesus said not to sacrifice this. Therefore, we must choose people who have a good testimony and are filled with the Holy Spirit to carry on this ministry of service."

The relationship at this stage is not only a relationship with God, but also a relationship with family. Usually this is where family relationships become very important. A leader looks back and asks, "What have I done with my family? Did I really give enough attention to my children, grandchildren, family, my wife or husband? What did I do?" In previous stages of leadership, a leader can be simply striving on behalf of the ministry so he can show his accomplishments at work. In this stage, leaders desire to show the value of their relationships at home.

This is when most leaders, particularly in Christian ministries, regret the time they neglected to give to their families. The regrets come, but sometimes for leaders it's too late. There is not much they can do at this stage, especially if they are advancing in years. The guilt still comes.

One day I was in the office of a Christian who is well known throughout the world. I arrived early and his assistant let me sit in his office while I waited for him. He walked in and closed his office door. Tears filled his eyes and he said to me, "I've lost my children." (At that time, one of his sons was going through a divorce.) There was total silence. After a few minutes he asked, "What could I have done differently?" This man was at the value stage, in that he was getting ready to enter a deeper relationship with others – and this time, including his family.

The value stage helps a person balance the relationships between God, family, calling or work, and ministry. The human relationships are not only those defined by family, but also those defined through common effort in the Kingdom. The emphasis shifts from viewing people around you as employees or followers, and seeing them as co-laborers. It puts a new value in the leader's responsibility to them. It adds importance to how the leader acts towards them.

In early leadership, during the reality stage, and even sometimes at the maturity stage, people aren't valued much. They simply "exist," and we work together. In the value stage, they are strongly valued. The leader asks, "Did I minister to them, or did I only use them to accomplish things? Did we just work together, or did I take time to minister to them? Did I make a difference in the life of a brother or sister who's working with me or partnering with me in the

Stage 6: The Value Stage

Kingdom work? Did I make an impact on the life of that person? Did I care? Did I show love? Can I say like Jesus, *'Haven't you seen God the Father? How do you ask me to show you the Father? Didn't I show the Father through my life example?'* (John 14).

These are the questions asked at this stage. The issue of relationship becomes very strong and important.

These are the questions that Wess Stafford began to ask around Compassion, too.

God had been showing Wess some hard truths about what kind of leadership was needed to lead the international ministry of Compassion to the next stage. At that point in his own leadership journey, Wess understood well his need for others to help him further define and deliver those values to Compassion's ministry around the world.

Wess began by taking those around him into a period of reflection. "We reflected on the past, and defined the values that had shaped us. We looked at the present, to gather a sense of what values were truly driving us to do what we did. And then we looked to the future, to come up with the values upon which we could both honor God and build Compassion for a new era.

"One of the first things that came up was my need for sound relationships with those serving with me. God had gifted me differently than any past president of Compassion. More than any other, I truly needed others to lead with me. I needed to develop a team based on shared values. Turning that corner took almost three years.

"While I worked on building a team, the team took on the task of defining the values that would shape history for our ministry and the children we serve. Our Board of Directors rewrote our mission statement to state a stronger challenge for us to serve the church, and for the church to serve children. We wrote out our commitments to those who fund our ministry and labor with us.

"We shifted away from a mindset that asked, 'What would the president do?' to one that emphasized 'What should *we* do based on the values we share?' We encouraged more strategic thinking. We took on problem-solving as a team. We established parameters for decision making, so more people could be free to make decisions."

Wess found himself taking on the role of counselor and mentor more frequently as the Compassion team developed. It was all a part of reinforcing the shared values that were emerging in the ministry – and taking on a role that goes with the value stage of leadership.

Chapter 12

Passing on Values

The value stage leads a person into a parenting role. It's like fatherhood, not in the sense of a biological father, but in the sense of bringing others into this stage and helping them become what God intended them to be – that is, being a spiritual father and discipling others.

One important aspect of this role is seeing the potential in others. This is exactly what was required of Wess as he developed the people around him: "As much as possible, we try to develop the potential in the people already engaged in Compassion's ministry. The effort has resulted in a lot of 'homegrown leadership' and younger leaders – both of which we feel is a benefit to the ministry."

The leader in this "fatherhood role" looks at the potential in young people and desires to bring out that potential by living an exemplary life. He takes time to disciple, work with and relate to them. He provides a covering for those he develops.

This is where the apostolic ministry comes in. One becomes a protector. The apostolic fatherhood is not only guiding, discipling and helping; as what Paul did for Timothy, Moses for Joshua, Elijah for Elisha, and Jesus for the Twelve. Being a father, in the apostolic sense, is to provide a covering, and includes correction, guidance, trust and being an authority figure.

This comes from that desire for relationships. At this stage a leader values his relationship with God, family, co-workers and others. This leads into the third stage of desiring to be a father: investing in others, giving what God has given to you to others so it's passed on. It involves viewing oneself as a provider and father in continuing the work of God, and discipling others to continue that work in your absence. In other words, laying the foundation to "work yourself out of a job."

Wess Stafford puts it like this: "My greatest joy is that the organization is less and less dependent upon me. My plane could go down, and Compassion would not only go on, it would go on well."

A second aspect of the fatherhood role is to give those around you "experience on the mountain." Let's turn to the example of Moses. Moses became a spiritual father to Joshua. Joshua served Moses. He walked with him, and Moses trusted and encouraged Joshua. He gave him responsibility. But even more important, Moses took Joshua with him to the mountain of the Lord where Moses had a relationship with the Lord. He took him to the mountain of God, to the presence of God, where Moses spent time before the Lord. In true discipleship, a father figure takes young people to the presence of God, where God manifests His presence and where the holiness of God is.

What makes this aspect so important is that it shows the relationship a leader has with God. On their trip to the mountain, Joshua observed what kind of relationship Moses had with God.

The third aspect of the fatherhood role is that of helping others discern events and God's voice. If we continue with the account of Joshua and Moses on the mountain, we'll discover that Moses helped Joshua interpret the sound they were hearing when they came back to Israel's camp from the mountain. Joshua thought it was a cry; Moses knew it was a celebration. It was a celebration of idolatry, as the Israelites were worshiping the infamous golden calf. So

Joshua was near Moses as they both processed the experience of the holiness, purity, majesty and glory of the Lord on the mountain, *and* the contrast of what human beings were doing without God, with their rebellious hearts.

That was true discipleship. It was the fatherhood relationship: First, time with God; next, looking at the people together. Joshua then observed how Moses dealt with the scene or situation. Joshua was observing and watching. Joshua was at the tent all the time. He was faithful. He served the Lord in this situation. Moses, as the father figure, knew when Joshua should go with him to the mountain, when Joshua should be at the gates of the tent and when he should come and observe when Moses dealt with sin.

The fourth aspect of a leader's fatherhood role is prayer coverage. Later on in this story, Moses went to the top of the mountain and sent Joshua to war. While Joshua fought, Moses' task was to pray for him (Exodus 17:8-16).

There's a time to go with a disciple to war and a time to just send him. Moses was praying for Joshua and for victory. Joshua was fighting. That's what fatherhood is, discipling and protecting. The protection of Moses was over Joshua. When Moses straightened his hand, he had victory and success. When Moses put his hand down, Joshua lost. That, symbolically, was Moses' covering or protection over Joshua's efforts in battle.

The Lord Jesus did a very similar thing for His disciples. After the great miracle of feeding the multitudes, He sent the disciples across the lake while He went to the mountain to pray for them. When they had to face the waves, He came to help them at the right time. This is the key to fathering. (Matthew 4:13-36) Another time He sent them two by two, with authority, to spiritual war (Luke 9, 10).

Another important aspect of the fathering role in leadership is to lead others into full responsibility. This is crucial in preparing the ministry to go on in your absence (either temporary or permanent). Joshua had been well prepared for leadership. He was ready to succeed Moses when the time came. He had years of practical experience and a history of seeing God work in and through his mentor, Moses. God affirmed Joshua as Moses' successor to Moses several times before Moses' ministry was finished.

That led to another aspect of the fathering role of a leader: the imparting of godly character. Moses did it for Joshua over a period of years, culminating in a blessing described in Deuteronomy 34:9: *"Now Joshua son of Nun was filled with the spirit of wisdom because Moses had laid his hands on him. . . ."* Jesus repeated this pattern through His investment in His disciples that culminated with the impartation of the Holy Spirit (John 20:19-23).

More than this, the Lord Jesus also did something in the discipleship process, or the fatherhood relationship, that is the final aspect we want to discuss now: he showed the value of loving His disciples. Jesus answered their questions, revealed the Father to them, prepared them for future ministry and also served them.

Remember John's account of the Last Supper? In chapter 13 of his gospel, John records that the Lord actually washed the disciples' feet. He extended His love, until the end, to those whom He loved. Jesus washed their feet, in spite of their weaknesses. Peter denied Him three times the same night. Thomas would later doubt Him. Judas was just waiting to betray Him. He had already sold Jesus, and was waiting for just the right time to give Jesus over to His enemies. Others doubted and were in great fear. Some were arguing amongst themselves who would be the greatest in heaven. In spite of this, He didn't rebuke the disciples for their sins, but He knelt before them and washed their feet. That was a relationship. That was being a father.

It's the promise of God that leaders are to be fathers to others, preparing them for life, washing their feet, correcting their weaknesses, strengthening them, encouraging them and lifting them up. And this happens in the value stage. In a leader's life, the value stage is the time for investing in discipling others to become fathers to others who are in the discipleship process.

PASS ON A PATTERN

Another characteristic of the value stage is to pass on a pattern for ministry or a pattern for life. David did this for his son Solomon. In 1 Chronicles 28, David gives advice to his son. He passes a value on to his son, so his son will be successful in his ministry and walk with the Lord. In fact, David asked the Lord to give him a pattern so his son wouldn't make a mistake. David talks about that pattern in 1 Chronicles 28:19: *"Because the hand of the Lord was upon me, he gave me understanding in all details of the plan."*

David gave a pattern to his son. The greatest issue at the value stage is not passing on responsibilities or inviting a person to a position of succession. While these are good, they aren't enough without a pattern. David didn't only give a throne, and through ceremony say to his son that he was going to make his son a king after himself. He asked the Lord to give him a pattern for the house of the Lord. A pattern was needed. God gave him the pattern and showed him what the house of the Lord was to look like. Then he received it in writing from the Lord.

What a fantastic thing! So he wouldn't make a mistake, David asked the Lord to give him the pattern in writing and the Lord did this. He received the pattern from the hand of the Lord. David passed it on to Solomon, his son. David said, "I received this from the Lord, and now you do it. Here is the pattern."

David shaped history by preparing Solomon to build the temple of God. Without David's input, it would have been difficult for young Solomon to build the temple – where the glory came down (I Kings 8).

In the value stage, this is what leaders or true fathers desire. They want a pattern to pass on. That's why, particularly in apostolic ministry, prophetic ministry, pastoral ministry and all of the five-fold ministries, having a pattern to pass on is extremely important. These offices are given to equip the saints for the work of the ministry. How can we equip the saints for the work of the ministry without providing a divine pattern?

God has a specific pattern for every generation. The message of the Gospel is the same, but the pattern or the way God wants to move varies according to the generation. In fact, one of the challenges of being a father and discipling others is asking the Lord for the pattern for that generation and passing it on. This is to ensure that the generation that builds the temple will not make a mistake. When leaders do that, the glory of the Lord, being revealed in the name of the Lord, is usually honored and praised. Young people are thus equipped and prepared for the work of the ministry, and will have a positive impact on the kingdom of God by advancing the Kingdom.

And what will that pattern include? Wess Stafford has noted, "Leadership must share *values* and *vision*. Both must come from God. They will form a pattern that anticipates where a ministry must go in the future."

PRACTICAL ADVICE

There are two points of practical advice that Wess has worked into the everyday fabric of Compassion, as well. "It is crucial that we operate with practical integrity in everything from our relationships to our accounting. We also advise that everyone be as professional as possible with the responsibilities God has given them in this ministry. To give that advice 'feet,' we also equip the people in our ministry with the personal and professional tools they need."

That kind of practical advice is also part of the value stage of leadership. Paul's example as he mentored Timothy offers three aspects to consider in giving practical advice as a leader.

First, Paul deals with personal issues. He instructs Timothy to drink wine for stomach problems. By this Paul shows Timothy that he cares about his personal life as well as his ministry. He knew about Timothy's struggles and about the weak areas of his life. He was interested in Timothy personally, as his spiritual son. He knew about Timothy's family situation and circumstances.

Second, Paul is concerned with Timothy's spiritual wellbeing. He talked with Timothy and told him what to do if he served people. Paul gave him instructions on how to walk, and how to protect his personal life and walk with the Lord. Paul also covered the areas Timothy needed to grow in. In 1 Timothy 4:14, Paul said to Timothy, in essence, *"I encourage you to stir up the gift that has been given unto you."* Paul was there when they laid hands on him, and Paul also laid his hands on him. Paul encouraged Timothy to develop the gift that was released by God through the prophetic message. He was interested in Timothy's spiritual walk with the Lord. He was concerned how Timothy acted, how he led the house of the Lord and how he managed.

Third, Paul was interested in Timothy's leadership skills. He advised Timothy about a leader's character and management style. He gave insights on managing God's house, and what to look for in developing other leaders. He also told Timothy how to check himself on the issues of leadership.

Paul and Timothy's relationship was very deep, strong and significant. By the time Paul wrote the letters we have to Timothy in the Bible, Paul was ready to go home. But he told Timothy what to do, how to prepare and how to stand firm in the faith. Paul was his spiritual father. This is characteristic of a leader's value stage: training others for ministry, reminding others what it takes to lead well and giving personal life examples of your own experience.

Paul had finished the race, but he also wanted Timothy to finish the race. That's why he passed on practical advice to his protégé.

PASSING ON BLESSINGS

In the value stage, key leaders in both the Old and New Testaments passed on blessings to young people that God had invested in them. They weren't selfish in the way they blessed generations or how they passed blessings on. In the value stage there's a willingness to stop, reflect and pass on God's intended blessing.

A true and sincere leader not only passes on skills and "how tos," but also spiritual blessings. Jacob did this to all twelve of his children individually (Genesis 49). Moses did the same to the twelve tribes of Israel (Deuteronomy 33). We see this also in the ministry of Jesus. In Luke 24:50 it says, *"When he had led them out to the vicinity of Bethany, he lifted up his hands and blessed them. While he was blessing them, he left them and was taken up into heaven. Then they worshipped him and* returned to Jerusalem with great joy. And they stayed continuously at the temple, praising God."

This is the last blessing Jesus bestowed on His disciples. Before He left, He passed on the blessing. The Father had sent him, so Jesus had said to them, *"...as my Father has sent me, so send I you."* The pattern is the same. Jesus passed on the blessing.

That's why when the disciples went out and preached, the people said, "These men are from Galilee, from the countryside. They're not educated men." Yet they spoke with authority, and with the blessing. They brought forth blessings, such as healing and restoration to society. And the people recognized that these disciples had been with Jesus because Jesus had passed the blessing and authority on to them.

In like manner, the disciples passed on the blessing to the generation that followed them. The leadership was passed on willingly to the next generation. We must do the same. The blessing must be passed on to the generation we work with, and the generation we disciple as leaders.

SHARING THE AUTHORITY

Passing on the blessing also means sharing the authority. Moses passed on his authority over Israel to Joshua. Jesus passed on His authority with His blessing to the disciples. The disciples passed on their authority to others through the laying on of hands.

Why was this important? Leaders must be willing to pass the blessing, commissioning and spiritual authority on, so a person can go out and accomplish the purpose of God and fulfill God's will.

In today's society, it's known as "passing on a chair." In many cases, however, leaders aren't willing to even pass on the chair. Yet the value stage demands that we stop, reflect and ask, "What is really important here? What do I need to pass on?" The willingness to pass something on is ultimately what pleases God. This is what God desires in leadership.

Wess Stafford is preparing a time capsule to be buried at a ceremony celebrating Compassion's 50th anniversary. It will hold a list of the values that are shaping Compassion today. The intent is that the capsule will be dug up during Compassion's 100th anniversary, should the Lord tarry. "We want to impact future generations to do better than we're doing. We want them to better understand their past, so they can better shape the history of their generation, too."

LESSONS LEARNED

Wess is forthright about the lessons he's learned from his time in the value stage in his leadership journey. "The revolutionary aspect of the past few years has really been the shaping of our values based on a three-stage strategy: looking back, assessing the present and anticipating the future.

"This exercise looks simple on paper but remember the duck: It looks like it's gliding along without effort from the surface. But if you looked underwater, you'd see it's paddling like crazy. It was a greater discipline than we'd anticipated, but well worth the effort.

"An organization implodes if strategy is shared without sharing values, too. We couldn't afford to do that. So we acted on our need to develop and share values that we could build upon to the glory of God – and that meant we had to develop people and relationships, too."

WHERE CAN YOU GO FROM HERE?

In summary, at the value stage a leader develops a set of values based on his personal experiences and relationships with God and others. These values serve as a basis for ongoing maturity, as well as a filter for an ongoing reflection process. They also help a leader to be a father, discipler, advisor, and role model. These values challenge a leader to ask, "What is important? What is real?"

This is discernment. In the value stage, the leader enters into discernment or the wisdom of knowing what is and is not important. In this stage, a leader passes on values that will make a difference in the life of young people, in the lives of successors.

This is the value stage, through relationships or discipleship, and whether it's in a church or Christian ministry. A leader in the value stage stops, reflects, and says, "What have I learned so far? What can I pass on to the next generation? How do I shape history? What have I learned from history that will make a difference in the coming years?"

There are sets of values that a leader can pass on, as in what David did for his son and what Jesus did when He washed the feet of His disciples – and encouraged them to do the same for others. Both were passing on values. Ministry is not what people do for you. It's what you do for others. That's what Jesus communicated to His disciples.

Shaping history demands that you pass on values to people you have equipped – with God's blessing – to not only succeed you, but *exceed* you. It can happen with a prayerful walk through the value stage in the leadership journey.

QUESTIONS FOR REFLECTION

1. *Do you look forward to releasing the gifts of others, or do you feel threatened by it? Why?*
2. *"Building people" is a skill that is crucial in the value stage of leadership. But it is also important at every stage. What do you do each day to build those around you?*

As you see it, how would a leader's activities change if he/she focused more on the people he/she leads, and a little less on the work that surrounds them?

Stage 7
The Leadership Journey

I The Call
Process of >Hearing >Discerning >Promise >From, to and for

II Acceptance
Process of >Step of faith >Entering >Commission >Confirmation >Signs

III Early Leadership
Process of >History >Ministry >People >Team

IV Reality
Process of >Character building >Self discovery >Facing reality >Personal gifts >Call >God >Knowledge

V Maturity
Process of >Building Ministry >Recognizing offices >Correcting History >Making History >Shaping History

VI Value Stage
Process of >Relationship >Building people >Becoming a father >Bearing Fruit >Establishing Pattern

VII Relational Stage
Process of >Relationship >Leaving a legacy

VII Relational Stage
Process of
>Relationship
>Leaving a legacy

THE RELATIONAL STAGE

"When my glory passes by, I will put you in a cleft in the rock and cover you with my hand until I have passed by"
(Exodus 33:22).

In the midst of winter, I finally learned that there was in me an invincible summer.
– Albert Camus

The ultimate goal of any Christian leader should be to move into an ever-increasing intimacy with God. That intimacy is achieved in the relationship stage.

For the Christian leader, this stage can legitimately be considered a move "from glory to glory." The beginning of the leadership journey is likely to be remembered as being glorious, as is the anticipated ending.

Here is where a leader recognizes that which is of personal worth. The leader knows beyond question what he or she stands for, and what is worth giving your life to accomplish.

Jesus Christ moved into this stage early in life. For most leaders, this stage will happen much later. The marvelous thing is that it happens at all. This is where a leader leaves a legacy, a testimony for those who will come later. Here is where a leader makes clear that every effort was meant for the will, purpose and glory of God. The leader in this stage ministers to others not only through actions and words, but through life itself.

This stage is a time for:
- Reflection
- Deeper relationship with God and others
- Rejoicing in the success of others
- Shaping history by personal legacy

Take note of these themes as you read through chapters thirteen and fourteen.

Chapter 13

Come and Fellowship

The leadership journey is a process – a process that has a beginning and also has an ending.

In order to finish the journey well, a leader must be concerned with how he begins the journey or race. From glory to glory is the final stage, but in order to move from glory to glory, the starting point should be as glorious as the anticipated end. What makes the process of the leadership journey glorious at the beginning is complete understanding of the call of God and the holiness and awesomeness of the call of God. The call of God isn't just God telling someone to come and do something for Him. Rather, God is saying to a person, "I want you. I have selected you, have anointed and set you apart, so you are mine." He wants to accomplish His purpose through one's life.

When a person receives the glorious call of God, it's not a human call, neither is it an institutional calling. Rather it is a divine calling – the calling of God the Father, Son and Holy Spirit. When a person understands the glory, power and majesty of the calling, it will lead him to acceptance of the calling. A person who understands the awesome call of God accepts the call with humility and surrender to the will of God. That's what makes the beginning glorious. Understanding the intention and purpose of the calling, humbly accepting it, recognizing who God is and how much a leader needs to depend on Him makes this process glorious.

Once a person accepts the glorious calling of God, God says that He also is committed to the one called and gives to an individual or leader an indicator of His presence. Acceptance of the calling will lead to activity – moving into the office of the calling and acting in that office. We talked about the early stage in leadership where God uses success, struggles and fear – not to accomplish a task, but to build character in the life of a leader.

Early leadership is not the time to build a ministry, as much as a time to build the life of the one called to the ministry. This is what we see in the life of many leaders during the early stage. The challenges and hardships they go through is the character building process. During that time God affirms that He stands with the leader.

This leads to the reality stage. A leader is made aware of the reality of God, the challenges and his personal shortcomings. Coming through this stage demands a willingness on the part of the leader to be transformed. Then he can be used of God and molded into what God wants him to be. Once this stage is completed, a person surrenders to the working grace of God.

This brings a leader into the maturity stage. The process may involve a person going through a deep valley. The way to avoid this valley and move to the next step in the maturity stage is to stand on the promises of God. This means believing what God has said about the person, his calling, and the role God has for him. This is where knowing God is so crucial. The reality stage will bring us from knowing *about* God into knowing God *himself*. It's the time we know and understand God's character and attributes. It's standing on firm ground and starting to walk with the Lord.

When a person moves to this stage and starts walking with God they say, "Yes, I know my weaknesses, but will not surrender to them. I am surrendering myself to God, who is able to fulfill His purpose in and through me, and will lead me into the maturing process."

Stage 7: The Relational Stage

Spiritual maturity brings the reality of God forth and builds on the relationship of walking with Him. It helps one relate to and desire more deeply to do God's will. It minimizes selfish desires, fear of failure, personal reputation and building one's own image or one's own kingdom. Instead, it focuses on the kingdom of God, on surrendering to Him and the spiritual maturity of walking with God.

As this process continues it will bring a person into the value stage. Maturity starts producing value. These values answer the questions, "What is important? What do I live for? What would I die for? What's important to me?" As Paul said, "For me to live is Christ, to die is gain." In other words, "It doesn't make any difference. To live is Christ, meaning living for Him. To die is gain. I will be with Him. Today I'm willing to live for him, but if I die I'll be with Him. Therefore, I'm not afraid of death or of ministry, nor am I afraid of living my life." That is the maturity stage and will lead into the value stage.

At the value stage the person goes beyond himself. Maturity is what God is doing in the life of a leader. It shows how God is shaping a leader's life, character, attitudes, language, vision and mission. It demonstrates that God is using circumstances to build a person to accomplish what God wants. Once a leader passes this stage and enters the value stage, God starts producing something in that leader that can be passed on to others. The leader thinks, "The concern is not only me, but now also others. What can I contribute towards the success of others? My success and walk with God is not the only important issue: how can I help others so they can enter into the same kind of relationship?"

A leader's focus and priorities change before they start being responsible for the character and walk of others. A leader now isn't focusing on activities, but on keeping his or her relationships.

Relationships do two very important things in the life of a leader. First, they release a greater anointing on the leader. Obedience, a close relationship with God and daily walking with God releases a greater anointing in the life of a person as they walk with the Lord. That turns into the fruit of the Spirit. For a leader, the most important thing now is not whether the agenda is accomplished by the end of the day, but rather the degree to which he or she reflects the Lord Jesus Christ as they work through the agenda.

The leader now concerns himself more with the fruit of the Spirit than what he can do for God. This leads the leader into a greater concern for others: to being a father by caring, protecting and helping others grow. By helping both young and old, who aren't at this stage but need the same encouragement, a person becomes their spiritual father. This is not totally a matter of age, but it is a matter of maturity, values and being a father. As this value relationship continues, a person's personal walk with the Lord or his relationship with the Lord will also keep developing.

A person then will move to from glory to glory or into the final stage in their walk with the Lord. That daily walk with the Lord and fulfilling His purpose will lead a person into the seventh stage, the relational stage.

This is the final part of an individual's ministry. What must be emphasized here is that we are not talking about retirement. We're talking about the process. To reach this stage, from glory to glory, as they continue from the value stage to the glorious stage of walking and being sensitive to the will of God, might take a long time. A person may move into this stage early in the leadership process, but it doesn't mean the person is ready to retire or ready for death. For most people, this takes them almost to the end of their earthly walk. That, however, is not always the case.

The Lord Jesus Christ entered this stage early in His ministry. From glory to glory is what we see in Jesus Christ's life every day, exemplified by His walk with the Father. He said He didn't do anything that He hadn't heard the Father tell him to do. He didn't do anything that He hadn't seen the Father doing. Total commitment was there and He walked in that glorious relationship. It wasn't for personal reasons, but only for the will and purpose of God. That is the ultimate walk with the Father, for the will of God.

That's why the Lord Jesus could boldly say, "Here I am as it is written in the Book; I came to do your will." Everything the Lord did was written in the Book, according to the purpose and will of God. He didn't speak His own personal words; He spoke the word of the Lord. He didn't act on his own; He submitted himself to the will or the actions of the Father. He walked through this relational stage and it was a glorious walk.

Moving into ever-increasing glory and intimacy with God is the ultimate goal of the leadership journey. Therefore, Jesus didn't only minister to others, but He ministered to God himself. He ministered to people around him, not only through His acts and words, but through His life. That's why he could say, "Haven't you seen the Father, Phillip? Haven't you seen the Father? I am walking with Him. I'm covered with His glory. I'm with Him! Haven't you seen Him? I'm showing the Father in everything I do, and in everything I say." That was the journey of the Lord Jesus Christ.

Two of the leaders we interviewed for this book – Wally Erickson and Mulatu Belachew – are in this stage of the leadership journey. Wally has been retired from Compassion for some years and is enjoying an active personal ministry to others in this time. Mulatu is still actively employed by Compassion in Africa. Yet at this writing, he has already outlived the life expectancy of those born in Ethiopia. The realities of mortality and God's blessing have dovetailed in Mulatu's life to bring him to a point of true freedom in his relationship with Christ and others.

We'll continue at this point with a few reflections on this stage of deep relationships from Wally Erickson.

SHAPING HISTORY THROUGH MOLDED HEARTS

"There's a certain amount of trust that comes with the leadership journey. It comes when you feel God has anointed this whole process and you're assured of that. I think you have to run with the highs and the lows of the journey. You have to believe it's all going to work out because God's in it. So it isn't so much what we *do* in order to make it a success. God's going to help right it all and conclude it to His glory. Why? Because that's really His choice.

"To whom do you leave your legacy? I think we have to have that assurance, somehow or other, that we are investing in others that God is choosing for service to others. If we don't have that conviction, if we don't have that internal confidence, then obviously it's not a choice at all. But if we have that confidence, then I think we have to risk it. Do you understand that? *Risk it.* Because you may not be able to see how it's going to turn out and you may not understand how it's all going to come together in someone else's journey, but God does. And His plans are always better than ours. So is His ability to work in others.

"Because we live in a temporal world, we sometimes feel the only thing that shapes the world is a hammer; or clay that we can mold. It's got to be physical force with material. Some sort of matter. That's what we can work with and how we build houses. But humans aren't that way. That's why you come back to the heart. God works on the inside of man, not on the outside. It's amazing to me you can write policies and manuals, and say, 'Read this book; it will really help you' and actually believe that it will be enough to mold a leader. All those things are great, but they're not the Word of God that the Holy Spirit speaks through.

"A man who is disappointed and dejected and depressed and mad one day can be loving and sweet, and kind and obedient the next day. That doesn't happen through the physical world of trying to mold things that are material. It happens because God does His work in the man's heart. So I think if you're going to develop as a leader, you must consider whether you see evidence of God bringing about radical change within your heart from day to day. Not once at an altar, but on a routine or regular basis.

"Even in this stage of the journey, I think that God's calling has to be almost relived. Every once in a while I think, 'What am I supposed to do in this stage in life?' And I keep going back to the things that I know to be true.

"I would say that a man's heart, the very thing that qualifies him for godly leadership, can be his glory or his shame. Because a man with heart has feeling for people, sometimes he will not face the hard issues of life or the hard decisions of life. So when it comes to really taking a stand for something that's good, he might appear to waffle. He might appear to be weak. He might appear to put it off and not face it today. So, the things that we need and the things that are attractive and the things that God can use, also become the very things that can be stumbling blocks to us and difficult for us to get past.

"I'm convinced also that everything is done for the kingdom of God, and not to be signed and seen by the eye of man. I think that people in leadership sometimes are prone to say, 'Look at the building. Boy, we're successful because it looks great.' Or, 'Look at the graph. It goes straight up in cost efficiencies.' Or, 'Look at the baptism record. I'm successful because I now have a church of 5,000 believers.'

"None of those is a criterion for success in the kingdom of God. Sometimes the things that are most successful in the kingdom of God can't be seen or measured by the eye of man. So I think that a true leader has to get beyond the approval of others, beyond the standards that our culture or society or moment in history might lay upon our backs. That's tough, because we all like the approval of men. How do you get it? You get it, by somehow or other being successful in their eyes.

"I think part of this process is falling flat on your face. Then you might learn to say, 'It's not as important as I thought it was to get the praise of man.' Then you're ready to go. So I think that you almost have to be isolated from worldly ambitions, approval and praise. Why? Because sometimes making the really hard decisions will reap a great deal of criticism from other people. The hardest thing in the world is to look a need in the eye and be able to say 'no' to maintain a focus. And sometimes those moments are very lonely.

"I still ask God to constantly test the depths of my thinking. I want to see if growth is still continuing and the Holy Spirit is busy sifting the chaff from the grain, if the fire is being applied to the gold to burn up the dross. I want to see that process every step of the way. I don't think that God ever gets through with that process in life."

There is no doubt that the work of the Holy Spirit continues to teach and sharpen those who are committed to the leadership journey.

Chapter 14

Finishing from Glory to Glory

Wally Erickson clearly enjoys the blessings of the relational stage. He still seeks God for further refinement so he can enjoy a closer walk with the Master. He knows what is important to pursue, and necessary to let go.

There are others who refused to finish as well as Wally has. As we continue to examine this final stage, I want to begin by recounting a few of their examples.

Eli, an Old Testament priest, started his ministry gloriously and with the Lord. When his children arrived, he refused to obey God in order to please his children. As a leader, he had a calling from God. God never said He didn't call him, nor did He question Eli on his calling. God simply told him that what he was doing with his children was not right. Eli didn't respect sacrifices, worship or God himself. Instead, Eli was ignoring these priestly concerns to favor his children. Therefore, as Eli continued in this fashion, God made a decision to end Eli's personal ministry and the ministry of his children.

The Ark of the Covenant was taken while Eli was serving in the temple in his old age. Eli was blind and deaf both physically and spiritually. He had no idea that the Ark was at risk. God revealed how the two areas were related. Eli lost his hearing, as he didn't want to hear the Lord. He lost his vision, so he couldn't see what was coming. In the court of the temple, he lost his spiritual vision, the divine vision, before he lost his actual physical vision. His vision became weak. He could not see sin, or what his children were doing in the house of the Lord or in the court of the temple.

As Eli continued to lose his vision, he kept himself on a chair. He didn't want to bring Samuel in and say, "I can't keep up with my kids. They're doing evil things. Can you help?" Eli didn't say, "Samuel, God has called you, and since He speaks to you already, I want to father and disciple you." Eli didn't do this. He still held tightly to the chair. He lost his ability to hear from the Lord. He lost his vision to see what God sees, even within the temple court. Eli held onto the chair, which represented his position. He didn't want to turn around and repent. He became a stiff-necked man. When he heard that the Ark had been stolen while he was supposed to watch over it – and why – the Lord basically threw over his chair. As a result, Eli's neck broke and he died. It was sad that Eli didn't finish his leadership in deep relationship with God, his sons and Samuel. But when a leader loses his hearing and vision, won't repent and turn to the Lord, but still holds tightly to a possession without the anointing, the glory departs. This is what happens in leadership when a leader completely refuses to turn to the Lord. This is *from glory to disaster*. Failure!

Another example is Saul. He started his ministry gloriously. He was anointed by Samuel, just as David was. When the anointing came upon Saul, he had a new heart and a new vision. In fact, Saul was given a spiritual gift and started prophesying. He wasn't a prophet by calling, as he was called to be a king. Yet the hand of the Lord was upon him. God provided for him. The day he was anointed, Saul found his father's lost donkeys. He was able to return home and ministered there with the approval and anointing of God, with the favor of God on his life. Later, however, Saul didn't continue in the leadership journey. Like many others, when reality hit, Saul couldn't continue into maturity. The Lord finally declared that He had taken Israel from Saul and given

Stage 7: The Relational Stage

it to David. Saul didn't accept this graciously, but instead he started pursuing David with plans to kill and destroy him. The spirit of jealousy started controlling Saul. Instead of the anointing, an evil spirit started attacking his mind and soul. He entered a disastrous situation, instead of from glory to glory as a servant of the living God.

This also was true for Judas, one of the Lord's apostles. He was chosen, set apart and given the same chance as the other disciples. But he couldn't resist the temptation to steal, and he was lost. He started out well, but didn't finish the race. He didn't carry out his role.

There are others, however, who started gloriously and finished gloriously. Does this mean there weren't ups and downs in their spiritual walk? Indeed there were! But it was under the grace of God, and they walked with God. They committed themselves to the Lord. The Lord kept them, restored them and encouraged them. The Lord took them all the way to where He wanted them to be.

One good example, as leader of a nation, was Moses. He started gloriously with the Lord: with dedication, commitment and with patience. Then he led the people through the wilderness, without complaining. Though he sinned at one point, God still declared Moses His servant. God took him gloriously all the way. Though God didn't allow Moses to enter the Promised Land, Moses was able to look into the Promised Land from the mountaintop.

Then Moses went to be with the Lord. At this glorious stage, one of the things we see is that those who finish the race gloriously with the Lord have one longing: to be with the Lord. Towards the end, after he asked the Lord who would take over for him, Moses prayed only one thing, "*Lord, show me your glory. That's enough for me.*" (See Exodus 33.) Moses only wanted to be with the Lord. The relationship became very dear and precious to him. It didn't matter if he could go into the Promised Land or not. He said, "Lord, I just want to be with you. Show me your glory." The Lord said, "I will declare my name before you. I'll pass my goodness before you. I'll cover you with my hand."

The hand of the Lord was upon Moses until the last minute. What a glorious thing! What a blessing if a leader is able to say the hand of the Lord *came* upon them when they accepted the calling and started ministering. How glorious if a leader who is taking his last breath is able to say to his followers, "The hand of the Lord is still upon me in its glory and fullness! I can still see the goodness of the Lord! I can still hear the name Jehovah. He declared His name before me. God is merciful. God is almighty. God is holy. God is unchanging. God is awesome!" That is moving from glory to glory. That's how Moses, the servant of the Lord, finished his race and calling. This was the final stage, entering into the glorious stage.

We see the same thing in the life of Elijah. He walked with the Lord. After he served he said, "Lord, maybe it's enough for me." The Lord said, "No, not yet. You have to still anoint a king and a prophet who will replace you." Elijah did this. Afterwards, the Lord gave him another chance to continue walking with Him. He became a father to Elisha. He enjoyed being with the Lord, just moving and walking with the Lord. The Lord said, "Son, I'm not going to prepare a burial for you. I'm going to send a chariot of fire to pick you up. We have been walking together. We have been talking and fellowshipping together. You have always been concerned about my glory, my name, and me. Let's go together."

How glorious! God sent a chariot of fire at the end of His servant Elijah's ministry. Here's what we read in 2 Kings

3:11, "*As they were walking along and talking together, suddenly a chariot of fire and horses of fire appeared and separated the two of them, and Elijah went up to heaven in a whirlwind. Elisha saw this and cried out, 'My Father! My Father! The chariots and horsemen of Israel!' And Elisha saw him no more. Then he took hold of his own clothes and tore them apart.*" This happened as they were walking. This is always the glorious finish in the life of a servant of the Living God. He wasn't only walking with God. At the last stage, the last step he took on earth as far as his walk was concerned, God was still walking with Elijah. Elisha had to pick up and run after him.

Some leaders drop the ones they've been fathering and discipling too early. They leave them behind. They're no longer walking with them. Elijah was still walking with Elisha until the end, when the Lord took him. That's moving from glory to glory. It's finishing a glorious race. How glorious it is!

We see a similar situation in David's life. David prepared everything. When he was ready to go home the Lord said, "No, you're not going to build the temple for me. I'll give you a son." He asked the Lord to give him a pattern, gold, silver and other materials for the house of the Lord. Until the end, the focus for David was not on his own kingdom, but on the house of the Lord. He wanted it made right. He was still counseling and talking to Solomon, his son, when he suddenly went home to be with God. That's why the Bible declares, "*When David had served God's purpose in his own generation, he fell asleep.*" David completed the purpose of God, serving well the purpose of God in his own generation. Then he passed it to the next generation.

In his generation David established a standard of excellence. Everyone saw it. After this, God used him as a standard for measuring excellence, in serving and walking with the Lord, and in the way he used his authority for the purpose of God.

Finishing well is a concern of any leader, especially those who find themselves in the relational stage. Mulatu Belachew reflects on the lessons he has learned in this final stage of the leadership journey.

PRIORITIES TO REDEEM THE TIME

"In Africa, shepherds go out into the fields with several sticks to use against animals that might harm their flocks. Many carry five such sticks. Fighting with the first four is no big deal. They're expendable. But when they get to the fifth and final stick . . . well, you have to use that last stick with priority.

"Maturity is a process. Yet in the last part of the leadership journey, you become more intentional and focused on the success of those you will leave behind. Therefore you focus on their gifts. Your joy is in seeing others empowered to do what God wants them to do. You focus on the next generation to keep maturing leadership in process.

"The generation gap is not an age issue; it's a relationship issue. I walked to a lakeside not long ago with my son. He said, 'Thank you, Daddy' – and began pouring out his heart. His fears, struggles, hopes and visions came out. Our relationship made it possible.

"I encourage others who have seasoned leaders in their lives to take every opportunity to learn from them. We have ignored men and women of God who have served in God's house for years because they reach a certain age. We shelve them. We let TV take over our community wisdom. Even our elders have bought into this. But where are the Moses/ Joshua, Paul/Timothy, Naomi/Ruth and David/Solomon relationships?

"At this stage, God's Word takes on a new dimension, too. You read it with a mindset, a desire to know what God has to say to you today because you sense your time is limited. It's amazing what jumps off the page.

"You're more open to the Lord in this stage because you know your time is closing. Not long ago, I was actually depressed when I was thinking about the limited number of years likely left to me. It was then that God led me to Ephesians 5:15 and 16: *'Be careful how you live. Redeem the time for the days are evil.'* God let me know with that word that analyzing my life was good, but redeeming the time each day was crucial. How much time I have left is up to God. The important thing is that I know that the time I have left is the time God wants.

"Leadership, after all, is about recognizing what the Holy Spirit is doing *today*."

WHERE ARE YOU IN THE JOURNEY?

It is my prayer that we all finish the leadership journey well. Toward that end, I would like to examine three more leaders from the New Testament.

The Lord Jesus started His walk with the Father, and finished it well. At the cross the Lord Jesus said, *"Glorify your son."* The Father said, *"I have glorified myself through you, and I will glorify my name again through you."* He was referring to Jesus' death and resurrection. (John 12) The Lord Jesus submitted to the will of His Father from beginning to the end. When Mary and Joseph lost Jesus, they found Him in the temple. At the end, he cleansed the temple before going to the Cross. At the Cross, the curtain in the temple was torn from top to bottom. He served the Lord God and revealed the glory of the Lord. He paid the price and obeyed the will of His father. In His glory, while the disciples were watching Him, Jesus went to the Father in the clouds. He finished His ministry from glory to glory. He gave authority and power to the disciples to minister. He said, "*I tell you the truth, anyone who has faith in me will do what I have been doing. He will do even greater things than these, because I am going to the Father,*" (John 14:12). He was actually giving them a commission to do more than He did. This is a true leader. He prepares his followers to perform better than himself.

Something similar is seen in Paul's life. He had a glorious experience that he shared in 2 Corinthians 12:2: "*I was taken to the third heaven.*" He shared experiences, not only at the beginning, but also in the middle of his ministry. At the end of 2 Timothy chapter 4, he said to Timothy, "Timothy, I am ready to go home. I kept the faith and finished the race." This is how Paul described the conclusion of his journey: "*For I am already being poured out like a drink offering and the time has come for my departure. I have fought the good fight, I have finished the race, I have kept the faith. Now there is in store for me the crown of righteousness, which the Lord, the righteous Judge will award to me on that day—and not only to me, but also to all who have longed for his appearing,*" (2 Timothy 4:6-8).

What a glorious finish! That's the way Paul finished the race! He was not afraid to go home because he was just moving from one state to another, from one glory to another glory, as he was anticipating the final stage. He was to see and be with the Master. It's like finishing the race, stepping on the finish line, and then receiving the reward. That's how he finished his race.

Finally, we turn to John the apostle. He started his race with the Lord Jesus, accepted the calling, walked with the Lord, and ministered. Toward the end of his ministry while he was by himself, an exile for the sake of the cross of Jesus

Christ on the isle of Patmos, he wasn't complaining. (See Revelation 1.) He said, "*I was in the spirit, on the day of the Lord.*"

How glorious! John was moving from one glory to another glory. It was like the Day of Pentecost. John was in the spirit, the same Spirit that came upon them on the Day of Pentecost. He could have said it's similar to the experience they had on the Mount of Transfiguration when Jesus was changed before them, and they beheld His glory on the mountain. That beautiful cloud of His presence covered them. The voice came from heaven. After this, the hand of the Master himself came and touched the Apostles.

"It's the same Spirit, the same presence of God, although I'm on the island by myself," John could have thought. "Peter is not with me. James isn't with me. But the Master, the Father, Son, and Holy Spirit are with me on this glorious day of the morning of the Resurrection, when Jesus stretched His hand and said, 'Peace be unto you. I am the one.' It's the same experience that we had on the Day of Pentecost when the Holy Spirit came upon us like a fire and we went out witnessing. It was the same. I was in the spirit, on the day of the Lord. Then I heard the voice, the same voice that came to the lake when we were fishing and said, 'Follow me. I will make you fishers of men.'

"The same voice spoke again on the island and said, 'John, here is something I want to show you before you come home. I want to take you to heaven for a visitation. I want to walk with you on the streets of heaven, through the revelation. Let me show you my personality again, beyond what you understood while I was with you. In the spirit, let me show you who I am, the revelation of myself, and of the future; what the future looks like, and the revelation of heaven.

"I turned around to see the one who was talking to me. I saw the Church, the seven churches. The Son of Man was walking among the churches. Then I started looking at His hair. It was white. I started looking down. As I was going down from the top of His head to the feet, the beauty, majesty, and glory of who He is overwhelmed me. Though I knew Him, though I was in the spirit, it was too much for my flesh to take. I'm still in the flesh. I could not take the glory and majesty, nor was I able to stand. Then I was on my face, falling on my face, at His feet worshipping Him. I couldn't even speak. I couldn't say a word. I'm just on my face at His feet worshipping Him, giving him the glory, honor, praise and adoration He deserves.

"Then He put His hand on me and said, 'John, fear not. I am the one who died for you, who has risen. I am alive. I paid the price for these churches, for their weaknesses and shortcomings. I have a solution. I am the answer. Let me walk with you a little while before you come home. Let me show you what heaven will look like.'

"Then we went together for a walk on the streets of heaven, on the glorious streets in the New Jerusalem. We walked on the streets of heaven. We saw the glory. I saw the glory, majesty and power of what it looks like. Yes! I said, after all those glorious things, 'Lord, if you let me go back and leave me on the earth, please come back soon.' Jesus said, 'He who testifies to these things says, yes, I am coming soon. Amen.'

John finished his journey there, from glory to glory.

The question is, as a leader, where did you start? Where are you now? Where will you finish?

QUESTIONS FOR REFLECTION

1. *This stage is marked by preparing and leaving a personal legacy. That legacy is already being formed no matter where you are as a leader. In what areas of life are you building a legacy – and what are you doing to build a positive legacy?*
2. *What are you doing each day to build greater intimacy with God – a process that takes a lifetime?*

Describe in your own words how you wish to "finish" as a Christian leader.

Notes

Notes

Notes

Notes

Notes

Notes

The Leadership Journey

I The Call
Process of >Hearing >Discerning >Promise >From, to and for

II Acceptance
Process of >Step of faith >Entering >Commission >Confirmation >Signs

III Early Leadership
Process of >History >Ministry >People >Team

IV Reality
Process of >Character building >Self discovery >Facing reality >Personal gifts >Call >God >Knowledge

V Maturity
Process of >Building Ministry >Recognizing offices >Correcting History >Making History >Shaping History

VI Value Stage
Process of >Relationship >Building people >Becoming a father >Bearing Fruit >Establishing Pattern

VII Relational Stage
Process of >Relationships >Leaving a legacy

STRATEGIC LEADERSHIP FOR MAXIMUM IMPACT